PIONE__

LEADERSHIP

In Uncharted Waters

The most powerful strategy on earth

Harness unlimited possibility, potential and opportunity

Jonathan Blain

Amazing Authors

First Published in Great Britain 2018

By Amazing Authors

© Jonathan Blain

All rights reserved. No part of this publication may be reproduced, stored in or introduced into a retrieval system, or transmitted, in any form, or by any means (electronic, mechanical, photocopying, recording or otherwise) without the prior written permission of the publisher.

The right of Jonathan Blain to be identified as the author of this work has been asserted by him in accordance with the copyright, designs and patents act 1988.

This book is sold subject to the condition that it shall not, by way of trade or otherwise, be lent, resold, hired out, or otherwise circulated without the publisher's prior consent in any form of binding or cover other than that in which it is published, and without a similar condition including this condition being imposed on the subsequent purchaser.

Cover Design: Jonathan Blain

Jonathan Blain Logo – Paul Barclay, Dartmouth, Devon, UK

Illustrations: Presenter Media, Flat Icon Agreement ID I-7M80U-J4A03AM, (Other Copyright Acknowledged)

Typesetting: Jonathan Blain and Irfan Idrees

This book is not intended to provide personalised legal, financial, or investment advice. The authors and the publisher expressly disclaims any liability, loss or risk, which is incurred as a consequence, directly or indirectly, of the use and application of any contents of this work.

I don't own the term "Pioneering Leadership", although I do own the domain www. PioneeringLeadership.com. I accept that it can mean different things to different people and that others have already written about it. This book reflects my personal views about it; I want to make clear that my views may or may not be correct, true or useful. It is for you to make your own decision about whether you believe them to correct true and useful to you.

WHAT OTHERS ARE SAYING

"These are extraordinary times. The fourth industrial revolution, as it is called, is changing the way people live their lives and transforming the way business is done. It is telling that in this important book Jonathan only lists business leaders he admires who are founders. Those which broke out from the corporate structure. Not those which changed it from within. Why? Because that kind of change has not been required. Conformity, process, risk adverseness, in other words 'a safe pair of hands' is what was required. And once you get to the top why rock the boat? Not anymore. Jonathan set a course for liberation, creativity and bold authentic entrepreneurial leadership."

Lord Mark Price

Mark Price is a businessman, writer, speaker, consultant and former UK Government Minister of Trade. A former Managing Director of Waitrose, Deputy Chairman of the John Lewis Partnership and Chairman of Business in the Community, Mark has spent over thirty years unlocking the power of people in organisations. He is passionate about creating engaged and happy workforces, who in turn create longer-term sustainable success for businesses. His mission to nourish people and businesses, giving them the ideas and tools they need to flourish. He is a Pioneer, the author of multiple books including: "Fairness for All", "Six Steps to Workplace Happiness", "Workplace Fables and the groundbreaking tools Engaging Works.

https://LordMarkPrice.com https://Engaging.Works

WHAT OTHERS ARE SAYING

"The insightful book 'Pioneering Leadership in Uncharted Waters' by Jonathan Blain calls for leaders to be the driving force of progress, to venture into new creative ways or to bring into existence something revolutionary. This new concept is deemed to be what leaders of the 21st century need, a pioneering approach to authentic leadership development. Blain puts forth a new perspective of what leadership entails. Thus, the book is an essential reading material for leaders who are keen and enthusiastic to transform and elevate their organization to greater heights and achievements."

Admiral Kamarulzaman - Chief Royal Malaysian Navy

Admiral Tan Sri Ahmad Kamarulzaman joined the Navy on 24 February 1977 after completing his education at the Royal Military College. He took over as Chief of Navy on 18 Nov 2015. His previous appointment was as Deputy Chief of Navy. During the service, he held a number of positions in the Navy and Joint Services such as Chief of Staff Malaysian Armed Forces Headquater, Commander Joint Force in Kuala Lumpur, Fleet Commander in Lumut, Commander Naval Area 2 in Kota Kinabalu, and Assistant Chief of Staff (Plan and Operations) at the Naval Headquarters. His last service at sea was onboard KD JEBAT (FFG 29). He graduated from the US Naval Staff Course, Naval War College, Newport, Rhode Island as well as the Distinguished Graduate of the Fu Hshing Kang College, Republic of China in Political Warfare. He also attended International Surface Warfare Officer's Course at Naval Amphibious School in Coronado,

WHAT OTHERS ARE SAYING

San Diego. He was also a graduate of Principle Warfare Officer of HMS DRYAD, Portsmouth. He attended courses on International Crisis Management Course at the National Administrative Institute (INTAN), Kuala Lumpur and also various other military education programmes both locally as well as in Australia and the United States of America. He is a spokesman for the Maritime Security and participated in several seminars and conferences including the ASEAN Regional Forum (ARF) in India and Kuala Lumpur, US Military Operations (MILOPS) Conference in Singapore, International Maritime Organization (IMO) Conference in Jakarta, Littoral Defense Conference in Singapore, Electronic Warfare Conference in London and MIMA International Conference in Kuala Lumpur. He obtained his MBA from the University of Strathclyde Business School, Scotland and MA in Defense Studies and International Relations at the National University of Malaysia. He completed the Executive Program in Business Management in the year 2009 in the Kenan-Flagler Business School, University of North Carolina, USA. He has received numerous awards and recognitions from the Federal as well as the State Governments. He was the first person to have received the Chief of Navy Medal of Merit.

WHAT OTHERS ARE SAYING

"The earliest research findings around leadership and leader behaviour asserted that character and integrity were as important as capability in a leader. There is little doubt that being a fit for future leader, capable of dealing with the as yet unknown challenges, will require some, if not all the capabilities, described in this book. As a life-long learner, I am passionately curious about leadership and leader behaviour. Why would I eagerly follow one leader and not another, when on paper they were the same? For the last twenty years, I've been involved in researching and creating impactful leadership development programmes. Client's have described that leadership is no longer about just leading people; it is leading through change, uncertainty, transformation and technological advancements. More than ever before, leaders need to be the instigators of a culture of innovation and enable their talented people to thrive 'outside the box.' I truly believe Jonathan's new book "Pioneering Leadership in Uncharted Waters" fills a much-needed gap in the "fit for future leaders toolkit". I particularly like the clarity and simplicity of the Pioneering Leadership in Uncharted Waters Framework. I think Jonathan defines what the 'box' is and what people need to do to get out of it.

WHAT OTHERS ARE SAYING

I have known Jonathan for over 20 years, and it is perhaps befitting to mention we met as competing Skippers in the Cape Town to St Helena Yacht race in 1998. A fantastic 1700 mile adventure, and a measure of Jonathan's leadership, that of leading by example. Jonathan is a true thought leader and has the unique ability to translate his thoughts into practical and actionable pages, in his authoritative books. He is of the utmost character with unquestionable integrity, augmented by hugely imaginative capabilities. It is these qualities, which augment his pioneering leadership and motivate him to make a difference in the world".

Paul Bennett

Paul Bennett is the Director of Enterprise at Southampton Business School at the University of Southampton. He was recently voted in by the members onto the Board as a Trustee of the highly prestigious and acclaimed Chartered Institute of Management. He is an authority on Leadership, a professional speaker and trusted adviser to senior executives at major organisations. He's been involved with Leadership all his working life and seen it from many different sides, originally as an engineer and officer in the Royal Navy, then as a business owner, professional around the world yacht skipper, as an MD of an international business. For the last twenty years, he's been involved in leadership development both commercially and in senior positions at two leading business schools.

"*I started my working life as an electrician, and was part of the team that dug the first trenches for fibre cables in Iceland at the very early stages of the fibre to the home industry in 1998. I am now the CEO of Reykjavik Fibre Network, one of the world's most pioneering and ahead of the game wholesale open access fibre network companies, which has achieved almost 100% fibre to the home passed connectivity in Reykjavik, with gigabit (1,000 megabit) fibre connections to homes. If you live in Iceland, you'd love your broadband! I understand what Pioneering Leadership is like in practice including the good and the bad things. When I first met Jonathan Blain, I instantly recognised that he was different; he is one of the rare 1% who are natural born Pioneering Leaders, he is curious, visionary, insightful and a powerhouse of creativity and imagination. This book, Pioneering Leadership in Uncharted Waters, will set you on the right path towards breaking the mould and help you become a disrupting business leader. Being at the heart of the communications technology industry, I can say with certainty that the Fourth Industrial Revolution is well and truly underway, the speed of change is breathtaking, and I can see the results will be profound. I am proud to have an MBA, but I know that traditional leadership and management approaches need to adapt to this brave new world. The strategy in*

WHAT OTHERS ARE SAYING

this book offers unlimited possibility, potential and opportunity. Everyone will benefit from Jonathan's wisdom, we've all got a stake in the future and I agree with Jonathan that we all need to try to be a force for good, and using Pioneering Leadership can create a better future for everyone".

Erling Freyr Gudmundsson

Erling Freyr Gudmundsson is the CEO of Reykjavik Fibre Network. He is an entrepreneurial Business Leader, Thought Leader and Consultant, with in-depth knowledge and experience of Fibre Networks and Technologies, and expertise in IT / Telecoms and Data Centres. He was the 2018 winner of the Broadband World Forum People's Choice Award. His previous company Industria was named by CNBC European Business as one of the 50 key innovators among European companies and won a Red Herring.

WHAT OTHERS ARE SAYING

" Jonathan Blain's new book is important, relevant, and timely, because it teaches Pioneering Leadership and how to Break Out of The Box and new ways of thinking, and how to become a game-changer, which I believe is needed when the world is going through such troubled and turbulent times. I highly recommend it to business leaders and everyone who wishes to achieve more and create a better future. It is a truly ground-breaking book, and a 'must-read', in my view."

Arun Bedi

Arun Bedi is a humanitarian and peace activist and also the Founder & CEO of Indo British Consulting, a boutique management consultancy, whose origins go back to 1993, which works with major global corporations and entrepreneurial businesses, governments, investors including UHNWIs, supporting bilateral trade between Indo-UK, Indo-EU, and Indo-Africa and within the Commonwealth Nations and more recently fast-growing South East Asian countries.

www.IndoBritishConsulting.com

WRITE YOUR NOTES HERE

THE FOURTH INDUSTRIAL REVOLUTION

"We are on the brink of the Fourth Industrial Revolution. And this one will be unlike any other in human history. Characterized by new technologies fusing the physical, digital and biological worlds, the Fourth Industrial Revolution will impact all disciplines, economies and industries - and it will do so at an unprecedented rate".

"We need to develop leaders with the skills to manage organizations through these dramatic shifts. As professionals, we need to embrace change and realize that what our jobs are today might be dramatically different in the not too distant future. Our education and training systems need to adapt to better prepare people for the flexibility and critical thinking skills they will need in the future workplace".

Professor Klaus Schwab

Founder/Executive Chairman of the World Economic Forum

Pioneering Leadership is centre stage in the Fourth Industrial Revolution and the rapidly changing world; it is the driving strategy behind it, and can be your biggest friend if you embrace and use it, or your biggest foe if others use it to your detriment. What is certain, is that Pioneering Leadership is going to become an increasingly defining factor in the immediate and longer term future, in success or failure, and is going to impact all of us. The Pioneering Leadership Academy, this book, the Pioneering Leadership in Uncharted Waters Framework, and the deeper level Pioneering Leadership Program behind it, is designed to be part of just the new generation of education and training that Professor Schwab suggests is needed. It goes further, and also provides the framework for implementation and daily use.

The Fourth Industrial Revolution has arrived, and its impact is likely to be profound; we need to ensure that we use Pioneering Leadership as a "force for good", to create a better future.

"My concern, however, is that decision-makers are too often caught in traditional, linear (and non-disruptive) thinking or too absorbed by immediate concerns to think strategically about the forces of disruption and innovation shaping our future". Professor Schwab. He lists these things as elements of the new revolution:

1. *Implantable technologies*
2. *Our digital presence*
3. *Vision as a new interface*
4. *Wearable internet*
5. *Ubiquitous computing*
6. *A supercomputer in your pocket.*
7. *Storage for all*
8. *The internet of and for things*
9. *The connected home*
10. *Smart cities*
11. *Big data for decisions*
12. *Driverless cars*
13. *Artificial intelligence and decision making*
14. *AI and white collar jobs*
15. *Robotics and services*
16. *Bitcoin and blockchain*
17. *The sharing economy*
18. *Governments and the blockchain*
19. *3D printing and manufacturing*
20. *3D printing and human health*
21. *3D printing and consumer products*
22. *Designer beings*
23. *Neurotechnologies*

You'd do well to heed Schwab's warning, the sooner you can teach your people Pioneering Leadership, the better. The Pioneering Leadership in Uncharted Waters Framework provides you a clear, simple common framework you can use across your organisation.

DEDICATION

I dedicate this book to the small number of open-minded people who will dare to be different. People who will take themselves to and beyond the leading edge of progress, human endeavour and enterprise, to create a better future, and make a positive difference to themselves, other people, communities, countries, businesses or organisations and the wider world.

When you embrace pioneering leadership and achieve extraordinary things, you may inspire others, they may end up admiring you and looking up to you, but as it has been said before "No Guts No Glory". Pioneering leadership involves putting yourself on the line, embarking on endeavours where the outcome is uncertain, where others may also doubt you, criticise you, mock you, try to hold you back, push you off course and even resent you at times. There can, however, undoubtedly be nothing more inspiring, motivating and rewarding than to, make the seemingly impossible possible, solve challenging problems in unique ways, create and exploit exciting opportunities, compete against fierce competition and win and achieve extraordinary things.

Most people won't have the courage or the motivation to dare to pursue paths that are new, different and better; they will conform to the status quo and do what most other people do, which makes you special if you do.

Good luck in all that you do. Use the immense power of wisdom, love and imagination to guide you and help you to create a better future.

JONATHAN BLAIN — Moving The World

Extreme Game Changer   A Servant For Humanity

TRIBUTES

I'd like to pay tribute to all the Pioneering Leaders in the world, both past and present, who have achieved extraordinary things using Pioneering Leadership. I can't mention them all, but they include:

Business Leaders / Entrepreneurs

Richard Branson (Founded Virgin Group)

Bill Gates (Founded Microsoft)

Steve Jobs (Co-Founded Apple)

James Dyson (Invented Dyson Vacuum Cleaner and Dyson Group of Companies)

Ray Kroc (Founded McDonalds)

Thomas Edison (Inventor of the Light Bulb and more / Founder General Electric Company)

Mark Zuckerberg (Founded Facebook)

Jeff Bezos (Founded Amazon)

Larry Page / Sergey Brin (Founded Google)

Warren Buffet (Famous Investor)

Scientists

Marie Curie (Pioneering on radioactivity)

Alan Turing (Computer Scientist, Mathematician, Logician, Cryptanalyst, Philosopher, and Theoretical Biologist)

Niels Bohr (Physicist who made foundational contributions to understanding Atomic Structure and Quantum Theory)

Max Planck (Physicist - Quantum Theory)

Charles Darwin (Naturalist, Geologist and Biologist - Science of Evolution)

Leonardo da Vinci (Ultimate Polymath and Universal Genius)

Galileo Galilei (Polymath Natural Philosophy to Modern Science)

Nikola Tesla Inventor, Electrical Engineer, Mechanical Engineer, Physicist, and Futurist – Electricity Alternating Current)

Albert Einstein (Theoretical Physicist who developed the Theory of Relativity)

Isaac Newton (Mathematician, Astronomer, Theologian, Author and Physicist – Key figure in Scientific Revolution)

Engineers

Isambard Kingdom Brunel (Mechanical and Civil Engineer one of Greatest Figures in Industrial Revolution)

Archimedes (Greek Mathematician, Physicist, Engineer, Inventor, and Astronomer)

George Stephenson (Civil Engineer and Mechanical Engineer – Father of Railways)

Gustave Eiffel (Civil Engineer and Architect – Bridges, Railways Eiffel Tower)

Henry Ford (Pioneered Assembly Line Technique of Mass Production)

Elon Musk (Business Magnate, Investor, Engineer, and Inventor – Tesla Cars, Space X and more)

Burt Rutan (Aerospace Engineer Light, strong, Energy-Efficient Aircraft.)

Steve Wozniak (Electronics Engineer, Co-Founder Apple)

Fazlur Rahman Khan (structural engineer and architect, who created important structural systems for skyscrapers).

Country Leaders

Mahatma Gandhi (India)

Nelson Mandela (South Africa)

History is full of Pioneering Leaders; the most successful ones are remembered long after their deaths because they drove progress and in some way moved the human race forward. For each one who is remembered, there are countless more who are not, but who also made a difference, often a very big one.

Most people will never use Pioneering Leadership, because they will prefer to stick with the majority and with what they feel is safe. I mention these people to illustrate how nearly all the greatest people who have ever lived are Pioneering Leaders. If you are not one already, you can become one, regardless of what type of endeavour you are engaged in.

"There are Dreamers and Doers

Pioneering Leaders are the Dreamers Who Do."

TABLE OF CONTENTS

ABOUT THE AUTHOR

Jonathan Blain is a Pioneering Leadership Expert, an Extreme Game Changer, and a Servant for Humanity, who strives to positively change landscapes and move humanity forward. He is a professional speaker and bestselling author of 14 Books / $3.8m+ sales, whose work has been endorsed by many top leaders internationally. Previously a Royal Naval Officer, CEO of a Quoted Company and MD of a FTSE 100 Subsidiary, he is the Founder of the Pioneering Leadership Academy - A Leading Provider of Pioneering Leadership Education and Training, Coaching / Mentoring and Consultancy services to major organisations and senior leaders worldwide. He is the creator of the ground-breaking and easy to use Pioneering Leadership in Uncharted Waters Framework and Program.

Jonathan helps people to change landscapes, create better lives, careers, businesses and organisations, communities and countries and to create a better world.

Top leaders and thought leaders endorsing his work include nine heads of UK top 1000 companies, top leaders in the military and other organisations, and even an ex-president of a country. He has appeared many times in the UK and International media TV, radio and press. He consults and speaks at events and conferences around the world.

He is an advocate for peace and harmony, an agent for change and improvement, an opportunity creator and a visionary with powerful new ideas, and a belief that it is possible to make a better future when you embrace the New Enlightenment: the pursuit and use of Wisdom, Love and Imagination.

"When I was young and still connected to illusion and glamour, I used to like watching movies, and I decided I wanted to have the exciting, adventurous and rewarding life that I saw people in the movies having. I quickly realised that this life wasn't going to be laid on for me, so I set about becoming the author of my own life story, and director of my life movie. The result was that I gained considerable experiences, both good and bad. I experienced some massive highs and lows, had plenty of real-life adventures, made and lost millions, found myself in many life-threatening situations, including being shipwrecked in mid-Atlantic, and on more than one occasion reached rock bottom. I served as a Royal Naval Officer, worked for one of the worlds largest corporations for ten years, had multiple entrepreneurial ventures, including a joint venture with a UK top 100 business. I achieved a record-breaking IPO and served as a CEO of a Publicly Quoted Company for nearly five years and took on many varied consultancy assignments internationally. A massive curiosity led me on

About The Author

a journey of discovery; I wanted to understand many important things including success, happiness and fulfilment, the meaning and purpose of life, and how we can all make the most of our lives and our time on earth. I met and interviewed many top leaders from different fields, and I became obsessed with performance, success, improvement, enlightenment, meaning and purpose and the maximisation of possibility, potential and opportunity. That journey led me to an epiphany that transformed my life. I had a strong feeling that everything I had ever learnt, discovered, done, experienced and achieved, was part of a lifetime apprenticeship, to prepare me to help others on their life journey and to create a better future. My ego gave way to humility, as I discovered my destiny to become a servant of humanity, helping others.

I am most comfortable at the leading edge of Progress, Human Endeavour and Enterprise challenging the status quo. I specialise in finding world-class, innovative and creative ways of solving problems, delivering improvement and creating and exploiting opportunities, which help people to live better lives, have better careers, run better businesses and organisations and make the world a better place".

Jonathan was brought up a long way away from the sea in the centre of the UK, but from an early age, he developed a passion for the sea, boats, sailing and water, becoming a Royal Naval Officer and a keen yachtsman. Of all the Pioneering Leadership metaphors he could have used, his affinity to the sea, led to his choice to use the metaphor of "Pioneering Leadership in Uncharted Waters" as the title of this book and a label for his unique intellectual property and system about how to use Pioneering Leadership most effectively.

"Jonathan is an extreme game changer on the GC Index®. Our academic research on Game Changers, shows they are the ones who have the propensity to change landscapes and move the human race forwards, but they cannot do it alone. Game Changers see possibilities where others do not, often driven by frustrations with the status quo."

Nathan Ott, CEO of The GC Index

"Jonathan has …. yellow energy that high is off the scale imaginative… it is very rare to have that high yellow, the only other person I've seen that high is Richard Branson; it is a very imaginative and very much a mould breaker and game changer profile… its provocative in a positive sense, an agent of change/change maker."

Simon Wilshire, Founder of C-me Colour Profiling

Jonathan offers new thinking, new ideas and new solutions that positively change the status quo. The story of Jonathan's life and how he came to be one of the world's leading champions of Pioneering Leadership is at the end of this book; you can read it if you are interested.

"Pioneering Leadership is esoteric, I want to make it exoteric. It is the most powerful strategy on earth that unlocks unlimited possibility, potential and opportunity. It is available to you if you are brave enough to venture out the box into uncharted waters."

PREFACE
IN A NUTSHELL

In every field of human activity, endeavour and enterprise, including ones that you are involved with, there are a tiny number of people who lead the way, blaze new trails, disrupt, change the game and break the mould. They make a positively disproportionate difference to themselves and others, achieving the best results and outcomes, in the best way and gaining the best rewards, and bringing into existence what previously didn't exist; they are the Pioneering Leaders.

You might recognise them, they:

1. Can make the seemingly impossible, possible.

2. Can solve difficult and challenging problems in unique ways.

3. They can create and exploit exciting opportunities.

4. They can compete against tough competition and win, often against the odds.

5. They can achieve extraordinary things that other ordinary people can't.

6. They can create progress and even move the human race forward.

You can learn to do what they do, so that you too can achieve these extraordinary things, but to do so, you are going to need to overcome the extraordinary strong pull of conformity, which will do everything within its power to make you do what the majority (99%) of other people do. It will blind you to unlimited potential, possibility and opportunity and scare you into submission if you are not careful.

To be one of the tiny number of people (1% or less) who achieves the most extraordinary things, you will need to dare to be different, and break free from the incredibly strong shackles of convention and the status quo today, that will limit your potential and the opportunities and possibilities that would otherwise be available to you. Breaking free will be hard, but the prize will be worth it for those who do and succeed. Pioneering Leadership, the most powerful strategy available to humanity, is based on differential. For every hundred people involved in a similar activity, only one or less is likely to be a true Pioneering Leader. If everyone achieved what are perceived to be extraordinary things today, what was extraordinary would become ordinary, and the bar would rise; this is the way of the world; the bar is always rising. The Pioneering Leaders are the ones who challenge the status quo, who are ahead of the game, and strive for the best results/outcomes; they are the game changers, the mould breakers, the disruptors and the people who blaze new trails.

The need for new thinking, new ideas and new solutions has never been greater, with the world, individuals, organisations and communities on a knife edge between great opportunity on one side and huge threats on the other: economically, politically, socially, environmentally and at individual and organisational levels. Ask yourself these three questions:

- Can I afford to ignore the most powerful strategy on earth?

- Do I want to settle for lower aspirations, when I can have higher expectations?

- Do I want to be ordinary or extraordinary?

Pioneering Leadership has a massive impact on your life and the whole world whether you use it or other people use it; it drives progress and change which never stops. Remain blind to it or ignore it at your peril; it can be your greatest friend or foe.

Pioneering Leadership in Uncharted Waters™is a unique framework that is designed to help you and others you might collaborate with, to understand, use and gain maximum benefit from using Pioneering Leadership.

You might be familiar with the expression "Out The Box Thinking". The framework defines what the box is, a representation of the "status quo today" and "business as usual", and how you get out the box by using Pioneering Leadership, to create a better future.

Inside the box is where 99% of people operate, the "Non-Pioneering Leaders", it is based largely on knowledge and "the known" and the pursuit of "Best Practice". Pioneering Leaders (1%), by contrast, operate not only in the box, but also venture into "the unknown", "Uncharted Waters", outside the box, unleashing the immense power of imagination as well, which Einstein says is more important than knowledge.

Most Pioneering Leaders are natural, born Pioneering Leaders, but you can learn to use Pioneering Leadership even if it is not your natural preference, by either using it yourself, embracing Pioneering Leaders in your team, or hiring others to help you use it.

If you choose to embrace Pioneering Leadership successfully, you can harness infinite possibility, potential and opportunity and use the most potent strategy on earth.

Most organisations are Pioneering Leadership free zones; this benefits the 1% who use Pioneering Leadership because advantage comes from the difference between Pioneering Leaders and Non-Pioneering Leaders.

The power and potential of Pioneering Leadership is tremendous; use it wisely and as a force for good in the world. Every type of human endeavour and enterprise can benefit from it, from the smallest things to the biggest issues in the world.

There is a deficit of Pioneering Leadership education, training and support in the world, which this book, its author and the Pioneering Leadership Academy seeks to rectify.

At the core of the Pioneering Leadership in Uncharted Framework is the star, which provides a clear route "out the box", towards the infinite potential possibility and opportunity in the uncharted waters beyond. You've got to see, think, act, know and do differently to Non-Pioneering Leaders and become a Visionary, Innovator, Explorer and Adventurer. In effect, you deal with three variables, the Objective, The Options for achieving the Objective, and the Outcome actually received. You need to embrace imagination and creativity to the fullest extent.

Pioneering Leadership, may or may not involve leading others, organisations, causes etc; it could just involve leading yourself to a better place and better outcomes and leading by being ahead of others.

This book provides a high level overview of Pioneering Leadership and reveals its most powerful secrets; however Pioneering Leadership is a big topic and it is possible to achieve different levels of knowledge and skill. This book takes you to the highest big picture level.

The Pioneering Leadership in Uncharted Waters Program, follows on from the book and enables you to take Pioneering Leadership to a lower and deeper level and to apply it to an objective of your choice.

The arrival of the Fourth Industrial Revolution and the acceleration of disruption, makes Pioneering Leadership the most relevant skill needed by modern day leaders, to help them survive and thrive. The biggest challenge you'll face is getting to start working with Pioneering Leadership; most people will never get to step 4, taking action and using it.

Pioneering™
LEADERSHIP In Uncharted Waters
The World's Best Pioneering Leadership Framework

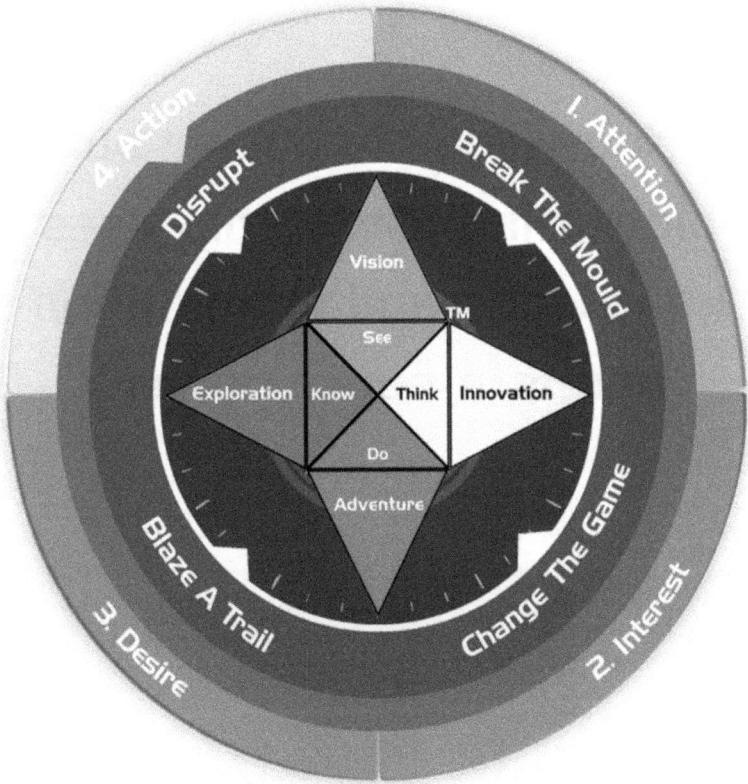

Never before have the secrets of Pioneering Leadership been revealed in such a clear simple way

Start From the Outside and Move Inwards Towards the Core

"Knowledge is power but pioneering leadership uses knowledge and imagination and is a super power."

Chapter I

Introduction

Pioneering Leadership – The World's Biggest Secret Hidden in Plain Sight

Chapter 1

Don't underestimate the importance of Pioneering Leadership; it drives progress, and without a doubt it is the most powerful strategy on earth, but for most people, it remains a massive and supremely important secret.

It is surprising, that even Pioneering Leaders themselves or others, rarely use the label "Pioneering Leaders" or recognise "Pioneering Leadership" as the cause of the outcome they achieved. It is like a big secret hidden in plain sight, that shows up pretty much everywhere. Many other labels may be used including: Humanitarian, World Leader, Statesman, Country Leader, Politician, Businessman, Entrepreneur, Sportsperson, Community Leader, Organisational Leader, Charity Leader, Military Leader or even just a talented individual with a specific area of expertise like Scientist, Engineer, Environmentalist, Artist, Musician, Peace Activist etc. Pioneering Leadership can make ordinary people great at whatever they do, and enable the greatest outcomes.

The simple truth is that we generally don't see the common thread, that runs through so many different people, well known and others, who have demonstrated the capability to achieve such extraordinary things. Pioneering Leadership might well have shown up in your life, and perhaps you've not even been aware of it? It is the opposite of business as usual and of ordinary regular approaches to anything. Pioneering Leadership is the thing that challenges the status quo.

Pioneering Leadership is like radio waves, you might know they are they are there, but you don't often think of them unless the need is great, like there is no mobile phone signal to make your call when you urgently need to speak to someone or you lose your WIFI connection.

Pioneering Leadership is arguably the biggest and most important thing that most people are not aware of. Even those who are aware of it, will mostly ignore it, dismiss it and forget about it. This response appears to defy logic, but supports the argument that as a species, we are not always rational; it might not be logical, it is most likely psychological, and an interesting feature of human behaviour.

Pioneering Leadership Offers the Greatest Possibility, Potential and Opportunity

Pioneering Leadership is the common thread between disparate people who achieve extraordinary things by being first, new, different or better; it is what Pioneering Leaders do, and it is The Most Powerful Strategy on Earth that contains the Greatest:

1. Potential.

2. Possibility.

3. Opportunity.

It enables you to achieve the best results and outcomes and the best rewards. It can be used across the entire spectrum of human activity and endeavour, to achieve virtually anything imaginable, from small and perhaps relatively insignificant issues at work or in your personal life, through to solving the biggest problems facing humanity. It can be used to tackle, poverty, food and energy shortages, pollution, global warming, curing and eradicating diseases and bringing about lasting world peace and prosperity for all.

What is most surprising is that until now, when this book was published, and the Pioneering Leadership Academy was founded, you'd be lucky to find anywhere where you could study and learn to use Pioneering Leadership for any purpose, so that you too could make the biggest difference and achieve the best results and outcomes and the best rewards.

It is mostly used by:

1. Natural Pioneering Leaders whose personality type makes Pioneering Leadership their natural preference.

2. People who have worked with or been influenced by Natural Pioneering Leaders.

3. People who have found themselves in extraordinary circumstances that have forced them to use Pioneering Leadership.

A Hidden Human Operating System

If you are familiar with computing, you may be aware of computer operating systems. Smartphones run on mostly Google Android, Apple IOS or Microsoft Windows operating systems. Hopefully most of the time our phones work, we don't think about how their operating system functions; we just accept that they do. We might install Apps (Applications) on our phones to do a variety of different things, from providing emails to GPS Navigation. From time to time, the operating systems will be updated, bugs and security failings will be fixed, and improvements made, especially when new hardware is available.

Without realising it, we each have our operating system, which resides in our brains. Our Brains enable us to live and our bodies to function as an integrated system. Somewhat like a computer operating system, it runs in the background and allows us to operate. During our lifetime, we learn skills, gain knowledge, develop unique personalities and characteristics and make choices.

When we learn something like how to ride a bicycle or drive a car, it can be stressful and tricky to start with, but eventually, the skill becomes second nature. Once we are competent at riding a bike or driving a car, we don't even think about it; we just do it, like we are on auto-pilot. What is more, we typically do it the same way, time and time again. Our brains are adept at learning habits; they can change, but like giving up smoking, or changing our eating and lifestyle habits to lose weight, it can be difficult to accomplish.

Our hidden operating system will cause the following:

1. Default Thinking

2. Default Beliefs

3. Automatic Responses

Given any situation, we are highly likely to refer to default thinking, default beliefs and automatic responses. Pioneering Leadership requires an understanding that these things apply to everyone, not just us. Take any group of people, and the chances are, that many of these things will be the same or similar. It is not difficult to predict how most of us are likely to react towards the same situation. In an extreme example, if we were unlucky enough to be somewhere where some lunatic was in the process of committing an act of terrorism shooting outside, we'd most likely run for our lives, because the fight or flight reaction is part of our human operating system. If you've had military or specialist training your first reaction might be to drop to the floor, then quickly move to better cover. Automatic responses are so critical that at times they can make the difference between life and death.

While thinking, believing and doing the same or similar things as most other people is often an excellent idea, it isn't always the case. Just because everyone thinks something, believes something or does something, doesn't make it right or good. For over 2000 years, when someone was ill, cutting them and draining off some of their blood, which is sometimes referred to as "bloodletting" was considered a good idea, to help people to get better. Now with the knowledge of modern science, we know that in all but relatively few circumstances, rather than being beneficial, it is very harmful.

Warren Buffet became the world's most successful investor by thinking, believing and doing often different things to the majority. Some people have made fortunes in economic disasters when many more have lost fortunes.

"We simply attempt to be fearful when others are greedy and to be greedy only when others are fearful". Warren Buffet

To gain benefits from Pioneering Leadership, you need to recognise that you and everyone else have a hidden operating system and that being different but better to others, involves changing and leveraging your internal operating system, to create better outcomes. It is unlikely to be easy because Pioneering Leadership means being unconventional. Learn to improve your personal or collective modus operandi, your operating system, and things you never imagined possible, can become possible for you.

There are just two principal human operating systems:

1. Pioneering Leadership which is used by approximately 1% of

the population.

2. Non-Pioneering Leadership which is used by 99% of the population.

Discover How To Harness The Most Powerful Strategy on Earth

Discover How to Harness Unbelievable Power in A Positive and Ethical Way

This book changes this status quo; it reveals the secrets of Pioneering Leadership, such that you can harness the most powerful strategy on earth and access the greatest potential, possibility and opportunity and make the biggest difference, achieve the greatest results, achievements and success and receive the best rewards. Whatever outcome or objective matters most to you, Pioneering Leadership can deliver the best; pick any opportunity, desire, need, problem, challenge, key performance indicator, issue, goal, you like.

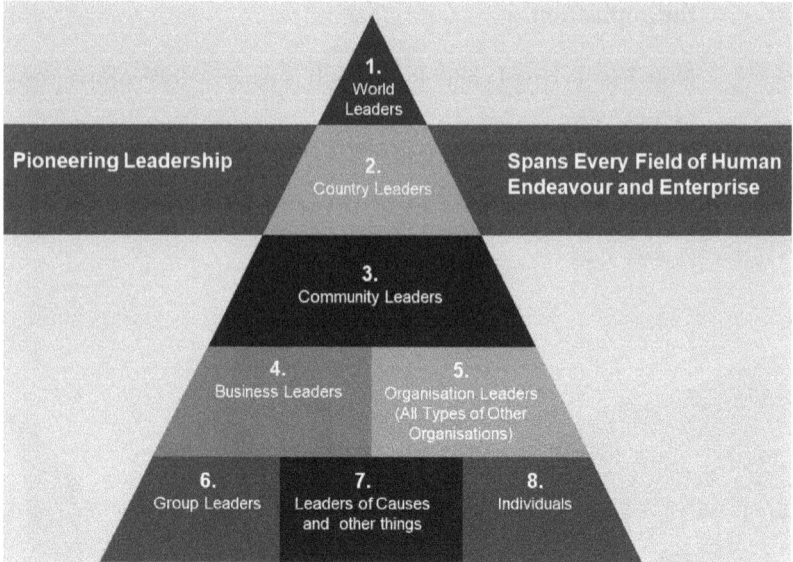

Pioneering Leadership Can Be Used By Virtually Anyone to Achieve Virtually Anything

You can use Pioneering Leadership to positively change your life, your career, your business or organisation, your community, your country or the whole world and all of humanity, and to achieve and accomplish things you probably think are impossible for you right now. What if you could solve huge problems, create extraordinary triumphs, achievements and success, or create and exploit the most exciting and rewarding opportunities imaginable, what would be the impact, what would you do, and how would it make you feel if you did it?

Most people presented with the truth that Pioneering Leadership is the Most Powerful Strategy on Earth are confused, disinterested or dismissive. Surely if it was the most powerful strategy on earth you'd know about it, everyone would be talking about it and would want to use it, it would be taught everywhere where performance and achievement is valued and important? There are many reasons that this isn't the case, the biggest being that there is an exceedingly low level of awareness about it. Given a choice to follow others or go it alone, most would follow others, regardless of the opportunity. With few people in authority of influence talking about it, it is going to remain a secret. People who use it for immense personal gain, don't want others, particularly competitors to know their trade secrets, or encourage them to disrupt them, so it remains largely hidden from view, and under wraps. Pioneering Leadership also invites users to challenge all that might be sacred to them; it threatens the status quo and can be seen as a threat to some individual's power, authority, security and sense of order. Huge power can be frightening as well as exciting! Just because something is not known, doesn't mean to say it doesn't exist; DNA existed, long before it was discovered. Given a choice between the known and the unknown, most people will opt for the known in almost any situation.

Pioneering Leadership – The Most Powerful Strategy on Earth

Powerful

Chapter 1

Powerful is: "Having great power or strength, prestige, or influence/control over people and events. Has a strong effect on people's feelings or beliefs or the outcomes of activities."

Strategy

A Strategy is: "A long-term / overall master plan, grand design, game plan, plan of action, proposed action, scheme, blueprint, programme, procedure, approach used to achieve a long-term overall aim/objective. Strategy is about you get from where you are to where you want to be in the best way, e.g. how to best get from A to B."

Pioneering Leadership is not that hard to understand, but it is something that is recognised and used by only a few people, but you can learn to use it if you want to.

Pioneering Leadership wears many guises and shows up in many situations; it is usually not recognised for what it is. For example, Pioneering Leadership attracts considerable attention when packaged for specific objectives, like "Disruptive Innovation", which was a concept created by American Harvard Academic, Clayton M. Christensen, which Wikipedia says has been described as the "most influential business idea of the early 21st century". Another example of Pioneering Leadership packaged is Blue Ocean Strategy, which is a marketing/business theory created by INSEAD professors, W. Chan Kim and Renée Mauborgne. The Blue Ocean Strategy book sold 3.6 million copies.

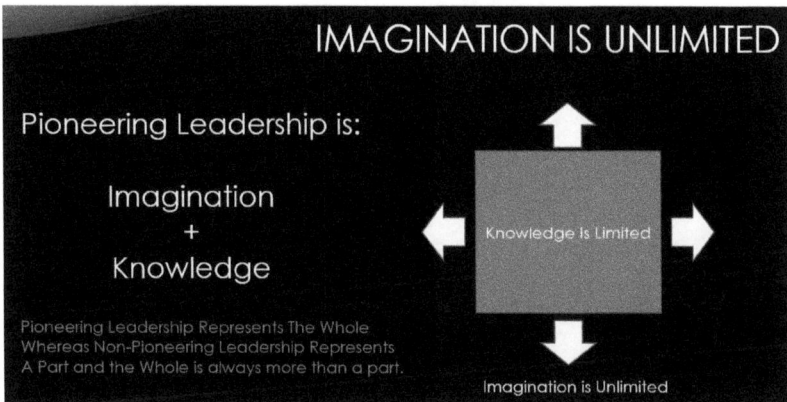

IMAGINATION IS UNLIMITED

Pioneering Leadership is:

Imagination
+
Knowledge

Pioneering Leadership Represents The Whole
Whereas Non-Pioneering Leadership Represents
A Part and the Whole is always more than a part.

Knowledge Is Limited

Imagination is Unlimited

Pioneering Leadership Embraces Knowledge and Imagination to Make It The Most Powerful Strategy on Earth

Chapter 1

The reason that Pioneering Leadership is the "Most Powerful Strategy on Earth" is because it fully embraces imagination, which Einstein says is more important than knowledge. By embracing both knowledge and imagination Pioneering Leadership offers the infinite possibility, potential and opportunity. It represents the whole rather than just the part, and the whole is always greater than the part.

To harness its immense power, you need to:

1. Recognise it.

2. Understand it.

3. Use it.

Think of Pioneering Leadership as a Tool in Your Personal Toolkit to Get Job Done in Best Way

A good way of thinking about it, is to see it as a tool in your personal toolkit that can help you to get any job done and achieve an outcome that you want and need. You need to use it in circumstances when it is the best tool for the job that you need to complete. A bad worker might blame their tools, but there is no doubt that the right tool for the job, can make all the difference, deliver a better result, quicker and easier.

Warning – Use Only as a Force for Good

Sadly, Pioneering Leadership is often the default for organised crime and terrorist groups like ISIS and Al-Qaeda. I urge you to only use Pioneering Leadership as a force for good. If you think about it, the extreme power of Pioneering Leadership was demonstrated by ISIS. According to CNN "ISIS is arguably the most successful militant group ever, seizing huge chunks of Iraq and Syria, declaring itself a state and governing territory for several years".

Chapter 1

Pioneering Leadership can be used for good or evil. My only concern in releasing its secrets is that some will seek to use it for pure greed, pure self-interest and for evil. I know it is a risk, but I believe that the urgent and important needs in the world coupled with a strong desire to only support the use of Pioneering Leadership as a force for good, makes the risk worth taking. I urge you to listen to your conscience and higher self in deciding when and how to use Pioneering Leadership. Having access to power in any form is a privilege and requires great responsibility. It is best used wisely in the service of others. At the very least, please don't use Pioneering Leadership to harm others or the environment, and always try to do the right thing morally. Please always bear in mind the possibility of unintended consequences. I recommend that you embrace the three tenets of the "New Enlightenment" in my book "Feel Good Change the World", which are the pursuit and use of:

1. Wisdom

2. Love

3. Imagination

Pioneering Leadership is the thing that enables underdogs in any situation to triumph, often against all the odds and the beliefs of others. Pioneering Leadership can deliver extraordinary results whether you want to use it for good or bad purposes.

It is much better we use Pioneering Leadership to improve things and to create a better future, solving the biggest problems and issues in the world, in our countries, communities, businesses and organisations and in our own careers and lives. If you become aware of people using it for bad purposes, please report them to the relevant authorities. Don't be tempted to use it to enrich yourself at the detriment of others.

I offer a variety of Pioneering Leadership related solutions, but I won't provide them to anyone I believe isn't going to use it as a force for good in some way.

Every decision we make and action we take has consequences, either positive, negative or neutral. Sometimes they impact only us, but other times they affect other people and indeed potentially the entire world. Many of the problems in the modern age, come from the fact that we have been blind to how we impact others and the wider world. For decades plastic as an example, has been thought of a wonder material, so much so, that it appears everywhere in our lives. We are now discovering vast quantities of it have found their way into the oceans with devastating environmental, social and economic consequences.

It is easy for each of us to think that we are insignificant and that the things we do don't matter and don't make a difference, or that just because everyone else is doing what harm we are doing it is OK, but that is simply not true. Today we all need to have moral backbone, a social conscience and be a force for good, and take responsibility for our own choices and actions. We need to care about the future and our responsibility to others and future generations. Why not try to the leave the world a little bit better than you found it?

Pioneering Leadership can lead to unintended consequences where what seems like something is good, like social media, connecting people, ends up also being used as recruiting and propaganda platforms for terrorist groups and a new means of bullying, hate spreading, illegal activity and communicating fake news etc. The Sunday Times Newspaper, talking about billionaire tech entrepreneurs (Pioneering Leaders) said: "their mindset is we're new and different. We're disruptors. We are free from the shackles of the past, especially regulation and government that stifle innovation. They see the world solely through a private sector lens". Profit often trumps what's right. Business success can come at a significant cost to others and the world.

It is not always easy to do the right thing; being human means having weakness and faults, it is normal, and none of us is perfect. It is, however, better to try to do the right thing, even if you sometimes fall short. Try to use Pioneering Leadership wisely.

Most People Are Not Interested In It – Why and What Does That Mean?

Most People Are Disinterested in Pioneering Leadership – Why?

Most people won't be interested in the contents of this book, not because it explains "the most powerful strategy available to humanity", but because it involves leaving the metaphoric Terra Firma, which represents "the known, the tried and tested, the proven, and the metaphoric path taken by the majority". Ironically it is the very lack of interest by most people, that enables the small number of people who use it, to achieve such profoundly significant and impressive things.

You'll love this book if you accept that you are here to stand out, not to just blend into the homogenous mass of humanity, and that you are also here to be all that you are and can be, and to accomplish all that you can, to make you feel most alive and fulfilled. The prospect of Pioneering Leadership should fire you up if you want to inspire and be inspired and are open to the possibility of being great and delivering great service to others, organisations and humanity, and being the best of who you truly are. Most people won't even consider or explore it.

Other people's disinterest in Pioneering Leadership means the possibility of huge advantage for you. It can help you to create progress, advancement and improvement and achieve extraordinary things. If you want to use Pioneering Leadership, it is brilliant news if most other people don't; if they did, it would make it significantly more difficult for you; the more disinterested they are, the better. Obviously, there are circumstances, like tacking the biggest issues facing humanity, where it is good news if everyone is interested in Pioneering Leadership and the most resources are put into solving the problems and creating and exploiting the best opportunities. Pioneering Leadership offers the possibility of significant advantage over others, which is good in some circumstances, like sport and anything that involves competition like business, the military, competing for jobs etc. Never forget, however, that we belong to one brotherhood of humanity, one life and are part of one world. How you use Pioneering Leadership matters, try to always use it as a force for good, this is a theme you will find repeated through-out this book. Try not be a luddite and at least consider Pioneeering.

The truth is that about 1% of people use Pioneering Leadership and 99% don't; it is almost as if nature makes it that way. How is it that nature seems to provide roughly the same number of women and men? Why is it also that 99% of the world's wealth is held by just 1% of the people? Except for a small percentage of noble philanthropists, it appears that most of the 1% with the greatest wealth, want to keep their quota. I don't believe there is a conspiracy of Pioneering Leaders, who want to keep their Pioneering Leadership knowledge and skills to themselves, I think it is more likely to be that most Pioneering Leader-ship is done by natural (born) Pioneering Leaders, where Pioneering

Leadership is their personality type. They are just being themselves.

It baffles me why more people aren't interested in the most power-ful strategy on earth, perhaps you have some ideas?

Seeing the Barriers Within That Hold Us Back and Limits What We Achieve

**Sometimes we put our own barriers in our way –
why don't we go beyond the line?**

Remember that the biggest thing you need to contend with, is the subconscious programming of your mind, which can hold you back, trap you where you are and deny you better things, and prevent you from using Pioneering Leadership. That might sound strange, but anything that asks you to challenge your core beliefs about things, to disrupt your default responses to situations and circumstances, that goes contrary to the way the majority of people see things, think and act can be hard, unless you are one of the few people who are already different to the majority.

The biggest barrier to the multiple benefits that Pioneering Leadership offers you, lie within you, they are not external to you. You can come up with lots of reasons why you can't or shouldn't use Pioneering Leadership, but you need to look inward to see yourself possibly as the real obstacle.

Natural Pioneering Leaders versus Non-Natural Pioneering Leaders

Few People Are
Natural Pioneering
Leaders!

You can learn Pioneering Leadership even if you are not a Natural Pioneering Leader

Are Pioneering Leaders born or made?

There are two variants of Pioneering Leaders:

Chapter 1

1. Natural Pioneering Leaders (Born)

2. Non-Natural Pioneering Leaders (Made)

Natural Pioneering Leaders – (Born)

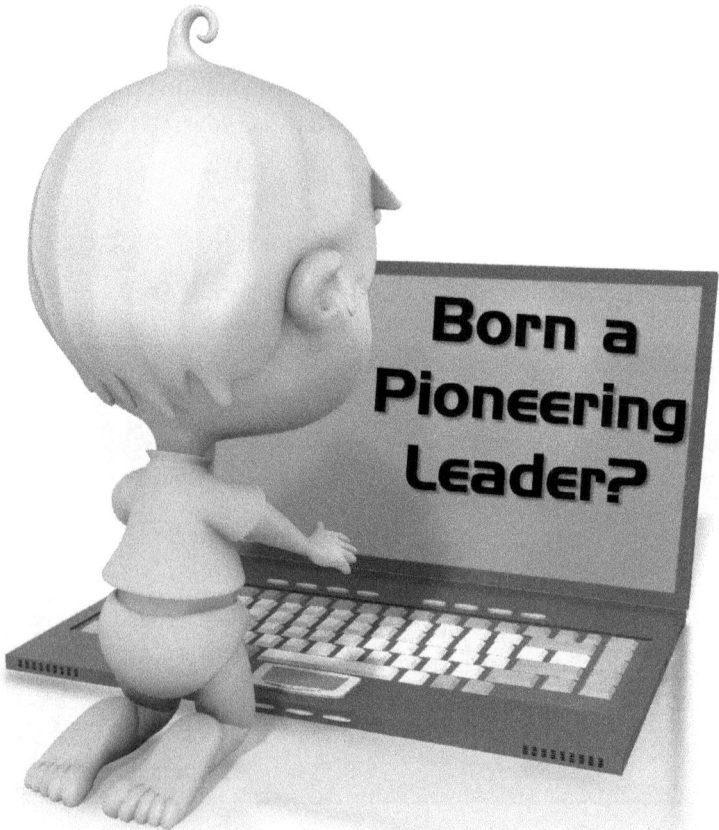

Most Pioneering Leadership is practised by Natural Pioneering Leaders, whose innate personality type and unchanging nature make

Pioneering Leadership their natural preference and modus operandi. They don't need to read a book on Pioneering Leadership or attend a training course; they just have to be their true selves and do what comes naturally to them.

Their default thinking and actions are those of Pioneering Leaders. If, however, they recognise what makes them different to others, they could identify and understand the possible friction with others that they may sometimes encounter, and also learn to refine, improve and enhance their Pioneering Leadership skills to achieve better results.

If the need or desire it strong enough, Non-Natural Pioneering Leaders can use Pioneering Leadership if they learn how to.

Non-Natural Pioneering Leaders – (Made)

It could also be that you are a leader who wants to try Pioneering Leadership; you might not want to learn to use it yourself, you want to learn how you can direct others to use it for you.

The Pioneering Leadership Framework/Model will help you to do all these things.

I think the jury is still out on whether Natural Pioneering Leaders are more effective than Non-Natural Pioneering Leaders. There are more of the former than the latter. Comparing the two is always tricky because each circumstance of Pioneering Leadership is different, so it is still a bit like trying to compare apples with oranges. Most people who are not natural Pioneering Leaders will struggle because they will feel outside their comfort zone. In contrast, Natural Pioneering leaders can be overconfident and so confident of their beliefs that they might not be so good at listening to others whose opinions are valuable.

Being a Natural Pioneering Leader can be tough, particularly when you are younger; you can feel different to others, but you would find it difficult to explain, and you might only recognise the consequences of being different, which might involve not being appreciated as much as others, being told off regularly for dreaming or not doing as you were told. You might be seen as the difficult one, questioning everything and frequently finding opportunities to go your own way. I understand this because I experienced these things. I didn't know I was a Natural Pioneering Leader then or how I was different to others, that only came in later life when I discovered assessment tools that showed me how and why I was different. Now I can help people shortcut to finding where their personal preferences lie.

Being in the minority means that you have no choice other than to function in a world where you are the odd one out, which usually means you need to learn to conform to the rules, beliefs and structures of the world, which are set by others.

I learnt to operate in the mostly Non-Pioneering Leadership environments of the military in the Royal Navy as a Royal Naval Officer, and within the Mobil Oil Corporation which was then the world's fourth-largest company. Challenging and questioning the rules isn't something you get to do very often in the Royal Navy; an organisation that is governed by rules (Queens Regulations for the Royal Navy), procedures, hierarchies and chains of command. If a senior officer says jump, you jump, you don't ask why, if the Captain tells you to alter course unless there are exceptional reasons not to do so like safety, you would do it immediately. Big corporations have lots of policies and procedures, limits of authority etc. you are likely to get sacked if you can't follow them or challenge them too often.

It was by learning to operate as a Non-Pioneering Leader when I am a Natural Pioneering Leader, that I discovered it is possible for all of us to do things that don't come naturally to us. While a Natural Pioneering Leader will be driven by instinct and preference to practice Pioneering Leadership, Non-Natural Pioneering Leaders can be taught what to do, and can also hire people who are Natural Pioneering Leaders to help them.

Fake Pioneering Leaders

Many Non-Pioneering Leaders, believe they are Pioneering Leaders when they are not. There is a psychological phenomenon that can make Pioneering Leadership, like innovation, seem cool and desirable. There is no Pioneering Leadership Police, exposing people who claim to be Pioneering Leaders, who aren't really. The Fake Pioneering Leaders are often the people who will push out, or hold back, block, or sabotage real Pioneering Leaders in their organisation. Many of the best real Pioneering Leaders are exceedingly open-minded and are often receptive to the ideas of others. Richard Branson is known to listen to other people and loves receiving great ideas from them that he can authorise and enable. Having a fake Pioneering Leader in authority can effectively block any real Pioneering Leadership taking place in their organisation and it can be hugely frustrating to others. Remember that you are only a Pioneering Leader when you are using Pioneering Leadership, no one can use it all the time. It is best to be honest.

"Pioneering leadership and non-pioneering leadership are both needed and important; they form an interdependent pair."

Chapter 2

Pioneering Leadership Versus Non-Pioneering Leadership

I estimate that only 1 out of every 100 is a Pioneering Leader

Chapter 2

To truly understand Pioneering Leadership, you need to put it in context with the opposite, which to avoid any ambiguity, is best described as "Non-Pioneering Leadership". Non-Pioneering Leadership is normal; it is what is practised by 100% of people, businesses, organisations, communities and countries approximately 99% of the time. Most Pioneering Leaders using Non-Pioneering Leadership most of the time.

There are many different styles of leadership in the world, but when it comes to the most important types, there are just two:

1. Pioneering Leaders

2. Non-Pioneering Leaders

Non-Pioneering Leaders account for an estimated 99% + of all leaders. Non-Pioneering leaders can be hugely successful, but they can never achieve the most extraordinary things, or access the greatest possibility, potential or opportunity that Pioneering Leaders can. They are traditional, linear and non-disruptive leaders.

Most leadership schools and leadership experts fail to extract pioneering as an important variant of leadership, probably because it opens entirely new realms, which involve more than just leading people, causes, organisations etc. which may include things such as:

1. Task Completion.

2. Planning and Visioning.

3. Goal Setting.

4. Blazing New Trails

5. Breaking the Mould.

6. Changing The Game.

7. Disrupting.

8. Invention, Innovation and Creativity.

9. Philosophy / Exploration / Adventure.

10. Strategy.

11. Performance Management.

12. Change / Transformation / Reinvention / Renewal.

13. Problem Solving.

14. Research and Development.

15. Operational / Project / Programme Management

16. Product / Solution Development.

17. Motivation and Incentivisation.

18. Competitive Advantage.

19. Attitude / Mindset / Beliefs.

20. Entrepreneurship.

21. Opportunity creation and exploitation.

22. Improvement and more.

Pioneering Leadership is holistic because its scope spans all factors that can impact outcomes and actions taken, where purpose and desired results are sometimes not known. Pioneering Leadership is like a big umbrella that covers many different things; as such it can be difficult to define and be able to say: "it is this" because it can also be other things too. It is probably for these reasons that, so few try to teach it.

There can be good and bad Pioneering and Non-Pioneering Leaders.

You need to understand that Pioneering Leaders represent a tiny percentage of all leaders/people, (1% or less), but they have a disproportionate impact on everything. Referring to the contribution of the relatively small number of RAF (Royal Air Force) Fighter Pilots in defeating the Luftwaffe of Nazi Germany, British Prime Minister, Winston Churchill made a famous speech where he said the famous words: "Never in human conflict has so much been owed, by so many to so few".

If Pioneering Leadership was widely recognised, which it is not, it would be possible to say something like: "In the entire history of humanity, a tiny number of people who are the Pioneering Leaders, have driven progress and had a disproportionate impact on the majority, both good and bad". Love them or loathe them, Pioneering Leaders are hugely significant to us all.

The Interrelationship Between Pioneering Leadership and Non-Pioneering Leadership

The world is full of pairs; these are just some examples:

1. Man and Woman

2. Day and Night

3. Hot and Cold

4. Introvert and Extrovert

5. Salt and Pepper

6. North and South

7. East and West

8. Positive and Negative

Two pairs that are rarely known but which are hugely significant to human existence, are "Pioneering Leadership" and "Non-Pioneering Leadership". There is a tiny percentage of Pioneering Leaders compared to Non-Pioneering Leaders. Precisely what that percentage is difficult to define, I estimate it to be less than 1%. I think the relationship between Pioneering Leaders and Non-Pioneering Leaders is rather like Yin and Yang, they go together and there is an interdependence between them.

Yin and Yang

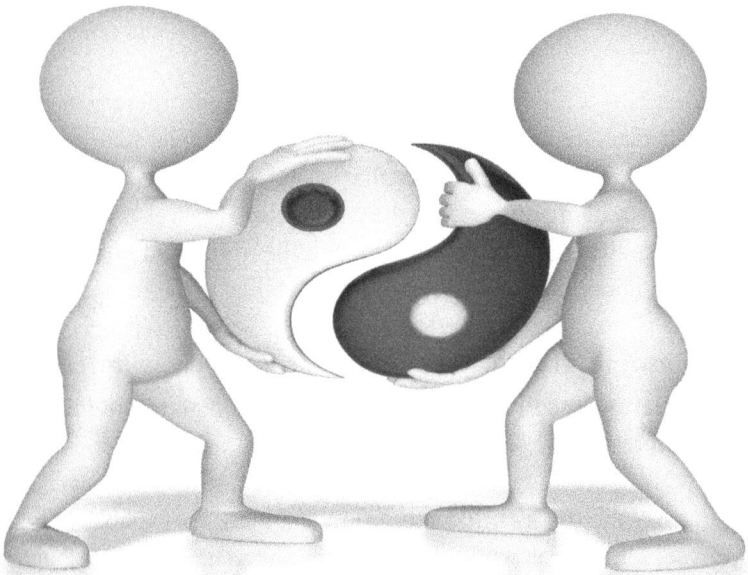

**Pioneering and Non-Pioneering Leaders Are an
Interdependent Pair**

Chapter 2

"In Chinese philosophy, yin and yang describe how seemingly opposite or contrary forces may be complementary, interconnected, and interdependent in the natural world, and how they may give rise to each other as they interrelate to one another. Many tangible dualities (such as light and dark, fire and water, expanding and contracting) are thought of as physical manifestations of the duality symbolised by yin and yang. This duality lies at the origins of many branches of classical Chinese science and philosophy, as well as being a primary guideline of traditional Chinese medicine, a central principle of different forms of Chinese martial arts and exercise as well as appearing in the pages of the I Ching". Wikipedia

Pioneering Leadership is only possible because there is a mainstream of Non-Pioneering Leaders / Ordinary People, that approach any endeavour in the same or similar ways. Pioneering Leadership is predicated on being different to the conventional mainstream. If there weren't a traditional mainstream, it would be much more difficult and probably impossible for Pioneering Leadership to deliver extraordinary results, because Pioneering Leadership would itself become the new mainstream. If this happened, the pair would disappear.

A society where Pioneering Leadership dominated would be chaos and would result in horrific anarchy. Having an organised society and world with controlling systems, rules and structure is massively important, but the truth is that these things are always capable of being improved, and that is where Pioneering Leadership works in harmony with the non-pioneering mainstream. In every endeavour, we need both a pioneering minority, transforming the future, creating new and better ways and things and a majority non-pioneering mainstream. They form as much an interrelated partnership and pair relationship as the other things mentioned.

The results of Pioneering Leadership endeavours that are highly successful, usually become the new mainstream. They quickly stop being extraordinary and become ordinary. This is the way of the world. When trains and planes and motor cars first arrived as shiny new results of Pioneering Leadership, they amazed people, whereas now we take them for granted because there seems nothing special about their existence.

Pioneering Leadership is the agent for invention, innovation, change, transformation, renewal and improvement.

Those who practice Pioneering Leadership need to take a humility pill and see that they are not better or more special than the mainstream, they are just performing a different role. In the bigger picture of humanity, both are needed, and both are equally valuable. However it is often the supremely successful Pioneering Leaders who gain the greatest wealth, fame, glory and recognition. Just look at the big tech company Pioneering Leaders to see this.

There are a small group of people who stand out as extreme Pioneering Leaders, who move the human race forwards, but even these people spend much of their time doing mainstream things. Many of the problems in the world come from the fact that we put ourselves into groups that separate us from people not in the same group. The groups could be anything we identify with, religion, racial type, nationality, profession, gender, sexual orientation, age, where we live, how much money we have etc. Having separated ourselves subconsciously we form opinions and beliefs, which might include whether we see ourselves and better or lesser than others. When we recognise that whatever differences may exist between us, we all human beings with the same basic needs, and that we all matter, the world will be a better place. Some Pioneering Leaders can be supremely arrogant and carry an air of superiority, and they really shouldn't.

Many years ago, I had an epiphany when studying psychology, I recognised that two people could see the same thing yet perceive it in different ways. I also understood that while we are all unique individuals, we are made up of physical, mental and psychological characteristics that can be categorised. While there is no one quite like you, or indeed anyone else, there are people who share many of our characteristics. Each characteristic has strengths and weaknesses, which means that our strengths can in some situations, have an equal and opposite weakness in other circumstances. It is for this reason that we all know that we are not suited at all to some jobs, where we are ideally suited to and comfortable with others. What is an excellent characteristic for one situation can be very bad for another. If a pilot of a passenger plane was a fearless risk-taker, who liked to live on the edge, as a passenger you would hardly feel pleased if he or she decided to play chicken with other aircraft to see who would move first, or who thought it might be fun to try and loop the loop to see if the plane could cope with it and test whether the wings would fall off. If on the other hand, they were to become a highly trained stunt pilot or fighter pilot specialising in air to air combat, they might be perfect for the job.

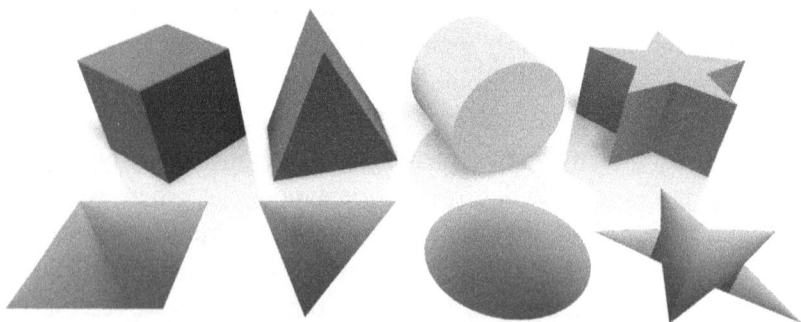

Everyone Fits Somewhere Best

An ideal world is one where we try to put square pegs in square holes and round pegs in round holes. We don't always recognise it, but the world needs all types, opposites give us balance and is a natural moderator.

Pioneering Leaders are merely people who use Pioneering Leadership. They are only Pioneering Leaders when they are using it. The truth is that anyone can use Pioneering Leadership, but some people have the personal characteristics that mean Pioneering Leadership is one of their main strengths; they are in effect Natural Pioneering Leaders because Pioneering Leadership comes naturally to them.

Even Great Pioneering Leaders Often Spend much time being Non-Pioneering Leaders

Even the greatest Pioneering Leaders and organisations, will spend large amounts of their time and effort involved in Non-Pioneering Leadership activities. The greatest Pioneering Businesses can't be Pioneering every aspect of their business all the time; if they did, it would most likely result in chaos, massive inefficiency and probably business collapse. I've never been to Tesla, or Dyson or Amazon or Google, who are companies that are known to be pioneers, but I am sure they have lots of regular, run of the mill, boring things that other organisations have too. At the very least, most organisations have to comply with many laws and rules; if they don't, the result could be anarchy and illegality.

Threats Facing Non-Pioneering Leaders

When you look at the some of the world's largest companies, you can see that it is possible for Pioneering companies to grow extraordinary quickly, but this growth would not be possible if these companies were also good at Non-Pioneering Leadership. Only a small % of leaders and employees of these companies will be Pioneering Leaders, and many of those Pioneering Leaders will be practising Non-Pioneering Leadership for considerable amounts of their time. A relatively small bit of Pioneering Leadership can have a truly profound impact. Equally Pioneering companies now present considerable threats to Non-Pioneering ones, with the average lifespan of an S&P 500 down from 60 years in the 1950's to under 20 years, according to Credit Suisse, and the lifespan trend looks set to continue its downward trajectory.

Non-Pioneering Leaders Are at Risk of Falling Off Cliff When Threatened by Pioneering Disruptors

Pioneering Companies, even small ones, can disrupt large Non-Pioneering ones, many of whom think they are Pioneering Companies when the truth is they are not. Often the biggest threats to organisations don't come from established competitors, but from the left of field, small companies, you didn't even see coming. There is a trend of cliff edge threats, where successful businesses can fail quickly like they have fallen off a cliff. This contrasts with the way things used to be, where tough times used to be a slippery slope, where will the right response, companies could check the slippage and decline and put themselves on a positive path of growth and increasing future success. Even if you recognise that you might be getting close to a cliff edge, it is hard to stop falling off at short notice; time is a precious commodity, and there comes the point where no more spins of the dice are possible, it is literally "game over". It is like an inevitable car crash, once the sliding has started, nothing can stop it, and the outcome is inevitably going to be the crash. It is one of the most horrible feelings because there is often little or nothing you can do to change the outcome and consequence is all bad. Being a Pioneering Leader is usually considered the riskiest type of leadership because you venture into the unknown, you don't know what you will discover or what the outcome will be; it might be good, or it might be bad. Our human DNA means we can't stand still, therefore it is only a matter of time before a Pioneering Leader creates something new or progress.

Pioneering Leadership is centre stage and more important than ever, because of what Professor Klaus Schwab, Founder of the World Economic Forum has called "The Fourth Industrial Revolution". "A range of new technologies are fusing the physical, digital and biological worlds, impacting all disciplines, economies and industries, and even challenging ideas about what it means to be human. This means that we live in a time of great promise and great peril". "My concern, however, is that decision-makers are too often caught in traditional, linear (and non-disruptive) thinking or too absorbed by immediate concerns to think strategically about the forces of disruption and innovation shaping our future". (Prof. Klaus Schwab)

The Biggest Companies in 2018

Company	Market Value $Billions Source: www.statista.com	Year Founded
Apple	926.9	1976
Amazon.com	777.8	1994
Alphabet (Google)	766.4	1997
Microsoft	750.6	1975

Company	Market Value $Billions Source: www.statista.com	Year Founded
Facebook	541.5	2004
Alibaba	499.4	1999

The Biggest Companies Today are Pioneering/Disrupting Tech Related Companies

Change is a constant which makes Pioneering Leadership forever relevant

We live in a world of continual change, and that change is one constant we can all rely on. Being alive today at this time in human history, means we need to deal with more complexity and more change than any previous generations. Change is likely to affect us, whether we like it or not. Pioneering Leaders are the initiators and originators of change, they might do it for pure self-interest or to create a better future for others. The real choice is where to be on the change curve. There are advantages and disadvantages of being in different places on the curve, every situation can be unique, and hindsight is often the only way of discovering if your chosen position was the right one.

Risk Versus Reward

Being first at anything can be great if you are successful and achieve an advantage, but sometimes effort and investment in time, energy and money can lead to failure. While there is always the positive of learning from mistakes, there is an apparent balance between risk and reward. Usually the less risky something is, the lower the potential rewards, but the more guaranteed those rewards might be.

The truth is that there are risks and rewards relating to both Pioneering Leadership and Non-Pioneering Leadership. At face value Non-Pioneering Leadership would appear less risky, the outcomes are more predictable and known, but in the long run, using it exclusively might be the highest risk strategy of all. As you learn more about Pioneering Leadership, you'll be able to form opinions regarding the risk versus reward arguments for both Pioneering Leadership and Non-Pioneering Leadership in your situation.

Uncertainty and the Merits of Pioneering Leadership over Non-Pioneering Leadership

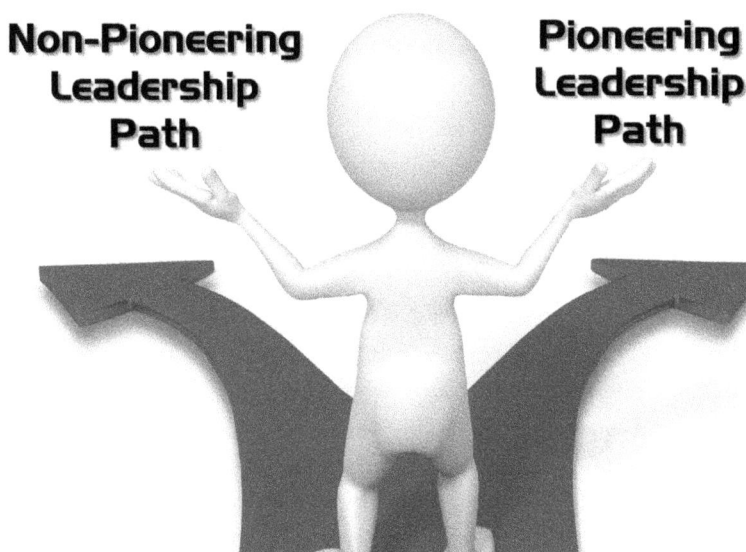

Non-Pioneering Leadership Path

Pioneering Leadership Path

The Non-Pioneering Leadership Path Isn't the Best One in Situations of Uncertainty

Everyone seems to agree that having crystal-clear goals and objectives is essential to achieve the most extraordinary things, yet that is often difficult if you are in a fog of confusion, full of uncertainty or just don't know which way to turn, what to aim for and what you should be doing.

Being agile and able to pivot quickly and effectively to respond to changes, challenges, threats and opportunities is one of the greatest skills and attributes you can develop; Pioneering Leadership enables you to do this. Despite this, most organisations and people are Non-Pioneering Leaders and are like supertankers when it comes to changing course; it is like they are on autopilot heading towards the next pre-programmed waypoint, milestone, goal etc., typically taking the same route as most others. Big corporations, with their bureaucratic structures, can be caught napping and can be disrupted by entrepreneurial start-ups and pioneering visionary competitors who change the game. Apple turned the music industry on its head, as Amazon did in the retail sector. Non-Pioneering Leaders are most likely to follow others, even if it is not the best thing to do, whereas Pioneering Leaders can often thrive in situations of considerable uncertainty.

Consider the fact that we live in a fast-changing world, where we don't know what might happen tomorrow let alone next month or next year, which means everything can change overnight. The financial crash of 2007 / 2008 demonstrated that entire countries were brought to their knees in a short period. Pioneering Leadership can be as much philosophy, a belief system and a guiding principle as it is a strategy of how to get from A to B. Entire ventures and endeavours can become quests and adventures when using Pioneering Leadership. You can use Pioneering Leadership to burn through the fog of confusion to anticipate the future, to second-guess the trajectory of things in your life, your career, your business or organisation, your community, your country and in the wider world, and to use your investigation and thought processes to create clear goals and objectives where none existed before. Often you need more than just a plan A and a plan B; you might well need a C, D, E, F and to create an entirely new one you hadn't even thought about if circumstances change. Luck sometimes plays a part, but you must be able to recognise, seize and exploit opportunities when they arise or else miss them.

Pioneering Leadership at the highest level is about creating a better future; you can't achieve that without addressing all three aspects: what, how and why. Simon Sinek in his book "Start With Why" created a good argument in the business world, for starting with the Why question. Whichever of the three you start with, you need to be prepared to look at the others and recognise that they are inter-connected and inter-related, change one and the others may also change. There is always a cause and an effect in play with everything. Pioneering Leadership can help you to achieve the best goals/objectives, the best motivations and the best strategies, and it is for this reason that Pioneering Leadership is more than just the most powerful strategy on earth.

Imagine going back in time and being a manufacturer of horse-drawn carriages and carts. No doubt there was at one time a massive demand for these. There would probably be many challenges to running such a business, that could occupy your thoughts and take your energy. When motor cars started to appear the market changed dramatically, things that might have seemed important before could well seem insignificant, when compared to a disappearing demand and a declining business. In more recent times, the music industry was turned on its head by Apple when it introduced the iPod, entered the music industry and changed the way in which music was bought and consumed. Think Uber, Airbnb, Facebook, Netflix, Spotify.

Pioneering small start-up low-cost airlines ended up taking massive market share, doing the same thing as the big established airlines, but only in a different way, i.e. with high efficiency, an obsession for lowering the cost and without the frills. Undoubtedly, teleconferencing stopped some people travelling at all, which in effect became a competition for the airlines. In due course, things like Skype, Facetime, WhatsApp and a plethora of other low cost and accessible tools killed off the high-cost teleconferencing business.

If you want to push the boundaries of possibility, change the game, create the best results or outcomes you need to put everything on the table that can help you. It is best to think of Pioneering Leadership conceptually from a big picture perspective as a way of creating a better future, not merely the most powerful strategy on earth. Pioneering Leadership can be your most significant friend if you use it yourself to your advantage or your worst nightmare if other people use it to your detriment. The lesson is "ignore it at your peril"; it is likely to influence and shape every aspect of your life in some way and at some time, because it creates progress, and we can't hold it back any more than we can hold back the tide. Pioneering is built into the fabric or human DNA; it is just used by the few, which influences/impacts the many. You must decide which camp to be in and when; the Pioneering Leadership camp of the few, or the Non-Pioneering Leadership camp of the many; it is a decision you must make about taking an approach of real leadership or abdicating to a default role of followership. There is a time and a place for both.

Examples of Pioneering Leaders

Albert Einstein Personifies Pioneering Leadership

Albert Einstein

With nothing but a humble pencil and paper and an extraordinarily inquisitive and powerful mind, scientist, Albert Einstein changed the world with his multiple theories and inventions including the famous theory of general relativity, which remains the single greatest contribution to our understanding of the Universe.

Einstein's discoveries had a far-ranging impact and led to the modern world that we recognise, with things like, laser beams, telecommunications, satellites, TV, Computer Screens / Monitors, Atomic Clocks, Atomic Power, GPS and countless other things that we now take for granted.

Einstein is accepted as one of the greatest geniuses to have ever lived, yet at school, he rebelled against the prescriptive nature of teaching, which resulted in some teachers giving him bad reports. His schoolmaster said: "he will never amount to anything". It took him two goes to pass the entrance exam to a Zurich Technical College, and he eventually graduated with only average marks.

While many others have taken his science, developed and expanded it, fewer have sought to understand, define, embrace and teach the underlying characteristics of his personality and behaviour that led to him achieving what he achieved, or to embrace the general wisdom that he offered all of us. Einstein was able to see things in ways that others couldn't, and used the immense power of his intellect, mind and humanity to rise above poverty, war and strife and become a shining beacon to mankind.

His journey to global fame was beset with struggle, failure and setbacks, yet it was arguably these things that drove him forward, increased his resolve and made him question his own beliefs. He had to overcome massive resistance to his ideas and theories, which overturned commonly held beliefs. At times, it was him against the establishment.

While Einstein is a truly unique human being; he is also the epitome of a "Pioneering Leader", who practices "Pioneering Leadership". It is arguable that his scientific genius and IQ alone, could not have enabled him to achieve what he did. His pioneering leadership attributes underpinned all that he did and all that he was. His Pioneering Leadership skills are far from unique, they are generic, and they have undoubtedly existed throughout human history, including today. Well known pioneering leaders of the modern age are Steve Jobs, Bill Gates, Warren Buffet, Jeff Bezos, Brin Sergey and Larry Page, Mark Zuckerberg, Richard Branson, Elon Musk, Oprah Winfrey and countless others well known and other. Pioneering Leaders can be found across every field of human endeavour in every age of humanity.

My proposition to you is that almost anyone can apply the principles of pioneering leadership to almost anything at all, once you learn what they are and how to use them. Natural Pioneering Leaders are born and pioneering leadership is a part of their personality type, there is no doubt about that, but the skills and process of pioneering leadership can be learnt and used to obtain the same or similar results by those motivated to do so.

Einstein didn't just leave a scientific legacy; he also emparted words of wisdom that reflect ageless wisdom. His whole life provides a role model and an opportunity to learn from every aspect of his life, both good and bad, and from his success and failures. He is a hero of mine.

What if you could apply the same principles of Pioneering Leadership that Einstein used in his science, inventions and life to your hopes, needs, desires and dreams and to issues in your private and work life?

It appears that Einstein is often misquoted, or quotes are attributing to him that he never said. The Ultimate Quotable Einstein book by Alice Calaprice does verify that Einstein said "imagination is more important than knowledge".

"Imagination is more important than knowledge. For knowledge is limited, whereas imagination embraces the entire world, stimulating progress, giving birth to evolution. It is, strictly speaking, a real factor in scientific research".

"When I examine myself and my methods of thought, I come close to the conclusion that the gift of imagination has meant more to me than my talent for absorbing absolute knowledge."

"Logic will get you from A to B. Imagination will take you everywhere."

"We cannot solve our problems with the same thinking we used when we created them." (Perhaps Not Einstein)

Elon Musk – The Epitome of the Modern-Day Pioneering Leader

Elon Musk (Photo © Steve Jurvetson)

Elon Musk is a billionaire, entrepreneur/business magnate, investor, engineer, humanitarian and philanthropist, and arguably the world's highest-profile modern-day Pioneering Leader. He is the Leonardo Da Vinci type polymath of our age, who changes the game and moves the human race forward.

Elon Musk is a great example of how Pioneering Leadership can be applied across multiple endeavours and enterprises. Born in 1971, Musk was listed by Forbes at the time this book was written to be the 53rd richest person in the world, with an estimated net worth of $20.8 billion. Wealth generation, however, is not his primary goal, which is to positively change the world and humanity, which resonates entirely with me.

Musk is not a business as usual guy, he is the absolute opposite, with fingers in so many pies and so many experiences and achievements, it is difficult to do justice to him.

He is best known for co-founding Tesla, makers of fantastic electric and self-driving vehicles and solar panels, SpaceX, which is an aerospace manufacturer and space transport services company, and for a company that became PayPal. He has multiple business and other interests, which include making humans an interplanetary species with plans to create a colony on Mars and reducing global warming through sustainable energy production and use.

He co-founded OpenAI, which is a not-for-profit research company that is interested in developing friendly artificial intelligence, and Neuralink, which is a neurotechnology company that specialises in developing brain-computer interfaces. He has plenty of other plans and visions including a high-speed transportation technology, the Hyperloop, and a vertical take-off and landing supersonic jet electric aircraft with electric fan propulsion, which is known as the Musk Electric Jet.

Elon Musk is a master creator, visionary, inventor and change maker.

Give Elon any problem, challenge or objective, and the chances are very high that he would be able to come up with fantastic, new thinking, new ideas and new solutions that offer the possibility of extraordinary outcomes. This was evident in July 2018, when twelve young Thai football players and their coach, became trapped by flood water approx. 2 miles into a subterranean cave network. Within days, Musk had created some innovative solutions to help rescue the boys, including an idea of building an inflatable tunnel and the actual production of a working child-size submarine, small enough to pass through the narrow gaps in the cave, and an offer of drilling expertise. While these ideas wern't used in the rescue; they could have been. Pioneering Leadership can be applied to virtually any situation, objective or goal.

While Elon Musk is supremely successful, pushing the boundaries of possibility, is not easy, and he faces continual setbacks in all that he does, many of which are high profile. For the last quarter of 2017, Tesla reported a loss of $675.4m (£487m) due mostly to Model 3 production problems, and in June 2018, announced shedding about 9 percent of its workforce, which amounted to over 3000 people. Pioneering Leadership is full of risk and uncertainty, and temporary or even permanent failure is always possible, but the prize when success is achieved, is frequently spectacular. Failure, challenges and setbacks are normal with Pioneering Leadership; it is not for the faint-hearted.

Tesla has been valued at more than both Ford and General Motors, despite being only founded in 2003. Pioneering Leadership challenges conventional rules. Ford and General Motors are huge compared with Tesla, they make millions of cars, while Tesla makes thousands of cars, and they make huge profits while Tesla has been making huge losses, but many believe that despite all that, Ford and General Motors are considered to be more representative of the best of the past, whilst Tesla is seen by many as most representing the best of the future, with vast potential that has yet to be realised.

There are plenty of warnings for big established companies who shun Pioneering Leadership and let the new innovators and disruptors take over.

Some people would love to be a Pioneering titan Leader like Elon, but being a Pioneering Leader is not easy and not without considerable challenges. Elon has publicly disclosed working 120-hour weeks, taking Ambien to get to sleep, and has even cried during interviews explaining how stress has taken a heavy toll on him in what he called an "excruciating" year (2018). Pioneering Leaders are often obsessive in their pursuits, which is one of the factors that enables extraordinary success, but there is usually a hefty price to be paid, physically and emotionally.

Musk himself said: "I don't think you'd necessarily want to be me - I don't think people would like it that much". He describes the inside of his head as like "a never-ending explosion" with ideas bouncing around all the time. He said he finds it "very hard" to turn his brain off". Natural Pioneering Leaders often live with idea-generating minds that don't turn off.

Just before this book went to press, the BBC reported at "The Securities and Exchange Commission filed a lawsuit accusing Tesla boss Elon Musk of securities fraud. The US financial regulator said Mr Musk's claims that he had secured funding to take the electric carmaker private were "false and misleading". As part of a settlement, Musk agreed to step down as chairman of Tesla and pay a $20 million fine, and Tesla greed to pay a $20m fine, to settle claims it failed to adequately police Musk's tweet.

The message has surely got to be a reminder that Pioneering Leaders might be able to metaphorically walk on water and achieve extraordinary things, but laws are laws and no one is above them. It looks from the outside that Musk has been suffering from almost unimaginable stress, we musn't forget that Pioneering Leaders are normal humans too, even if they sometimes appear like super humans. Pioneering Leaders often break rules and sail close to the wind, often there is a fine line between what is acceptable and what isn't.

Luddites

Luddites are people who dismiss Pioneering Leadership and won't even properly explore or consider its merits. Don't be a luddite!

Chapter 3

The Revelation

Pioneering Leadership Can Be Profoundly Significant

Chapter 3

Why You Should Be Interested in Pioneering Leadership

"A revelation is the disclosure of a surprising and previously unknown fact."

The existence of Pioneering Leadership is surprising to many people for whom it was previously unknown. It has been esoteric, which means "it is intended for or likely to be understood by only a small number of people with a specialised knowledge or interest". I don't know why that is the case, because the world needs it right now. I'd like to make it exoteric, so it can be easily understood and used by anyone with the need or desire to use it.

When explaining Pioneering Leadership, it is difficult to know where to start, because it has many different aspects and it offers the prospect of so many incredible and unbelievably good things. Please try to avoid jumping to conclusions about what it is and what it can do for you. Read the book and the many secrets and aspects will be revealed.

Pioneering Leadership is the Most Powerful Strategy Available to Humanity and More

Without a doubt, Pioneering Leadership is the Most Powerful Strategy on Earth. It can be used by almost everyone to achieve almost anything in the best way, delivering the best results.

It is the most powerful strategy on earth because it offers maximum:

1. Possibility.

2. Potential.

3. Opportunity.

4. And the prospects of the Best Results Possible.

The Promise - Definitions of The Three Things You Can Maximise

Maximise Possibility, Potential and Opportunity with Pioneering Leadership

Pioneering Leadership offers the promise of Maximum Possibility, Potential and Opportunity.

Possibility is a thing that may be chosen or done out several possible alternatives. The greater the possibility, the greater the number of alternatives and the greater the possible outcomes.

Potential is the latent quality or abilities that may be developed and lead to further success and usefulness.

Opportunity is situations that make it possible **to be** something, **to do** something, **to have** something, **to achieve** something, **to change, to improve, to transform** or **to create** something or an outcome or result that you want or need.

Chapter 3

Not a lot of people know about it:

1. Until now, it is rarely if ever taught.

2. You are unlikely to find it in the curriculum at even the top schools, colleges and universities.

3. There are very few books about it.

4. Virtually no one is searching for information about it on Google. In December 2017, there were less than 100 searches for it on Google in all regions

Sounds Familiar but Isn't

Pioneering Leadership sounds familiar like you know what it is, but very few people recognise it, understand it, know how to use it, and use it.

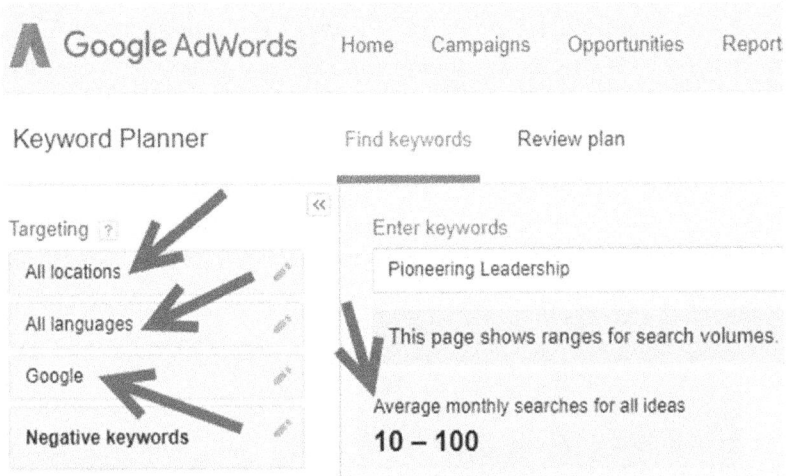

Pioneering Leadership Was Hardly Searched on Google in Dec 2017 (© Google)

At the time this book was written, the term "Pioneering Leadership" was hardly searched on Google with less than 100 searches in one month, in all languages and locations (December 2017) in all locations and languages. I had no problem registering the domain Pioneering-Leadership.com, which is yet another sign of how few people take an interest in it.

It is responsible for most of the greatest achievements in human history. These include scientific achievements, feats of incredible engineering, the most successful businesses of all times, the best organisations, countries, governments, civilisations, the greatest human endeavours, sporting achievements, military successes, the best social, environmental, political and economic breakthroughs etc.

Well-known Pioneering Leaders include Leonardo Da Vinci, The Wright Brothers, Albert Einstein, Bill Gates, Steve Jobs, Richard Branson, Elon Musk, Jeff Bezos, Thomas Edison, Nelson Mandela and Walt Disney.

Pioneering Leadership is used by most of the biggest names in almost every field of human endeavour, usually without them ever attributing it and often not recognising it. It is, however, not used by the clear majority of average/ordinary people, who are hardly aware of it.

Pioneering Leadership is everywhere, but it is frequently hidden in plain sight or invisible; it is very good at masking itself, and remaining hidden from consciousness, yet its impact can be jaw-droppingly awesome.

Contains Mystical and Magical Potential

Pioneering Leadership Can Make the Seemingly Impossible - Possible

It is the closest thing to:

1. Real Life Magic.

2. A Real Life Super Power.

3. A Magic Cure-All Elixir.

Real Life Magic

"It is important to remember we all have magic inside us".
JK Rowling

Have you seen the Harry Potter films, where Harry gets out his magic wand to make incredible things happen? Pioneering Leadership is like having a magic wand that makes the seemingly impossible possible. Who'd have thought a hundred years ago that humanity would have sent men to walk on the surface of the moon, or that ordinary people would be able to communicate at the speed of light or in the days of Concorde, fly around the world in luxury faster than the speed of sound? On an ordinary day, there is a city in the sky with an estimated one million people in aircraft above the surface of the earth. In the story of Aladdin, rubbing a magic lamp causes a genie to appear who offers to make wishes come true. Pioneering leadership doesn't deliver the outcomes on its own, but it provides you with the means to deliver results that might seem like they are impossible for you.

Super Power

"Often when we hear the word pioneer, we think of someone who we don't usually know, or just saw fleetingly on the stage before they went off to inspire another crowd. Someone who is a make-it-happen, person. Someone who blazes their trail and doesn't have a shred of doubt or incompetence but brings what others can only dream about into reality. In our minds, a pioneer is a superhero figure who, while breathing the same air as mortals, don't really let their feet touch the same ground. This thinking doesn't help us, because very few of us are like this, maybe one in a

hundred thousand. And because most of us aren't like this,
we assume it's just other people who can be involved in the
pioneering work."
Justin Welby – Archbishop of Canterbury

Imagine having a superpower as you see in the movies, where you can do incredible things that other people can't. If everyone has the superpower it will cease to be super; it would become ordinary and not extraordinary. Practising pioneering leadership is like donning a superpower cloak that enables you to achieve extraordinary things that others can't. You can use the superpower to accomplish a myriad of different things from curing diseases, creating love, peace, and harmony in the world, solving the biggest problems, creating the biggest opportunities, making companies and organisations successful, creating wonderful lives and careers and much more.

Cure All

"If a little dreaming is dangerous, the cure for it is not to
dream less but to dream more, to dream all the time".
Marcel Proust

Imagine having a magic elixir that could cure any problem, turn struggle, failure, setback or challenge into success, achievement or outcomes beyond your wildest dreams. Pioneering leadership is like having access to a magic elixir that is possessed only by the few, to make bad things good and good things even better.

It already is the thing that has the biggest impact on your life

It is the one thing that has the biggest impact on our lives because it is the principal driver behind progress and is therefore responsible for everything that progress has given us, including sadly the unintended consequences. Plastic, for example, was a seen as a wonder material, but now we are discovering that plastic is clogging our oceans, blighting our landscapes and causing untold harm. Social media that was meant to help us socialise has also enabled terrorists and paedophiles and people perpetrating hate and fake news and information and has created a mental health crisis. Everything that is normal today was once Pioneering Leadership.

Multiple Uses

Pioneering Leadership can help you to achieve:

1. Better Lives

2. Better Careers

3. Better Businesses or Organisations

4. Better Communities

5. Better Countries

6. Better World

Numerous Benefits

It can also help you to:

1. Make the seemingly impossible possible.

2. Solve difficult problems and challenges in unique ways.

3. Create and exploit exciting opportunities.

4. Compete against tough competition and win.

5. Achieve extraordinary things in whatever you are trying to accomplish or create.

6. Drive progress and move the Human Race forward.

Ideal for multiple circumstances

It is ideal to use in situations where you have:

1. Problems to solve, mainly if they are important and challenging ones.

2. Challenges to overcome.

3. A need or desire to create and exploit exciting opportunities.

4. A need or desire for the greatest success.

5. A need for desire for the greatest achievement.

6. A need or desire to make the biggest contribution.

7. A desire or need for change/transformation.

8. A need for improvement.

9. A need for relevance.

10. A need for survival.

11. A need for growth.

12. When you have uncertainty and don't know what to do.

Evolution and Revolution - Sustaining and Disrupting

People often associate Pioneering Leadership with radical revolution and disruption, but it is equally valid for evolution and sustaining as well as disruptive innovation. Sometimes the tiniest pioneering changes or inventions can make a huge difference that changes everything.

Can be used by almost anyone for almost anything

Because Pioneering Leadership is a high-level strategy, it is all-encompassing and offers a principle that can be used by nearly anyone for almost anything. This means that it is as relevant for world leaders as much as it might be suitable for you in your particular situation.

It is relevant for:

1. The Head of The United Nations.

2. World Leaders from the World's Biggest Countries and Other Big International Organisations.

3. Country Leaders.

4. Politicians.

5. Community Leaders.

6. Business and Organisational Leaders.

7. Leaders of NGO's, Not-for-Profits, and Charities.

8. Scientists.

9. Engineers.

10. People from all career backgrounds.

11. Sports People and People Involved in any Competitive Activity.

12. Ordinary Private Individuals.

Chapter 3

More than just the most powerful strategy on earth

The deeper you understand it, the more you'll discover, it is much more than just a strategy of how to best get from A to B; it is the ultimate game changer that can positively change everything.

It is many different things including:

1. A Strategy of how best to get from A to B and How to Achieve the Best Result / Outcome.

2. A Philosophy for Imagining and Creating a Better Future

3. A Means of Generating Goals and Objectives

4. A Means of Dealing with Uncertainty and Risk

5. A Means for Reinvention, Change, Transformation and Improvement

6. The ultimate performance realised.

7. Innovation in action.

8. Invention and creating what currently doesn't exist.

9. Infinite possibility, potential and opportunity.

10. Hope Made Real and more.

Pioneering Leadership is the Combination of Two Behemoths

Pioneering Leadership is merely the two behemoths of pioneering and leadership combined.

"Being First, New, Different and Better"

"Being Ahead of Others and The Game and Leading Yourself, Others and Causes to better places"

The Polar Opposite of Business as Usual

It represents the opposite of "business as usual", continuity and the status quo today. It is not just about the struggle to be better, it is about being the best and being first, and bringing into existence what doesn't already exist. It is not just about achieving the best results, it is about the discovering and using best method for achieving the best results and outcomes.

Normalisation - The Results of Pioneering Leadership

Pioneering Leadership drives progress, disrupts, transforms and leads to new things and extraordinary things. These things over time experience normalisation and become the new normal. Things we take for granted today were once cutting-edge Pioneering Leadership.

More than just innovation

A mantra of many CEOs is "Innovate or Die" and it is not hard to see why, with the average life expectancy of companies reducing and technological disruption being given as one of the major reasons. Being big and successful today is no guarantee of success tomorrow, you only need to look at the long list of previously successful companies that went to the wall including Woolworths, Polaroid, Alta Vista, Kodak, Blockbuster, Borders, Toys R Us, with many big-name brands in serious trouble.

All forms of innovation including Disruptive Innovation is a part of Pioneering Leadership, but Pioneering leadership is much more than just innovation. All pioneering is innovative, but not all innovation is pioneering.

Many individuals and organisations that are recognised as being innovative are those who are early adopters of innovations created by others, not Pioneering Leaders.

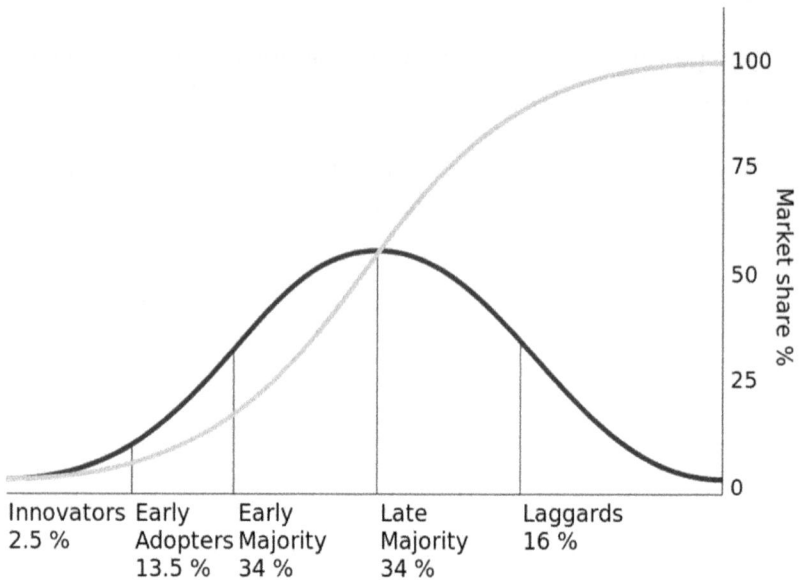

Rogers – Diffusion of Innovation

In American academic Professor Everett M. Rogers' diffusion of innovation theory, the group which is the first to try new ideas, processes, goods and services were called innovators and were suggested to account for just 2 ½% of the population/organisations.

Pioneers are the ones who create the new ideas, processes, goods or services in the first place. People often confuse innovators with pioneers. There is no "Definition Police" or authority, to arbitrate over these definitions, I hope that you can see the difference, and can use your sound judgement to differentiate. I suggest Pioneering Leaders account for 1% or less of the population. Providing hard evidence/research of the % of Pioneering Leaders in the world is impossible.

Chapter **4**

Changing Perceptions

Our view of the world starts in our mother's tummy

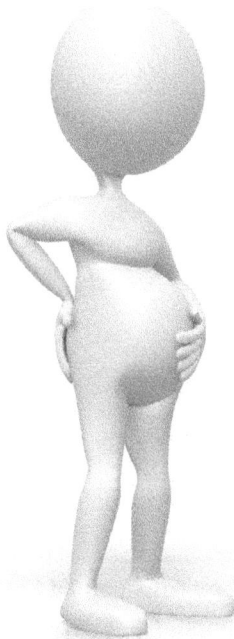

Before we even arrived into the world, we got used to boundaries

W e spend the first nine months of our existence inside a little womb in our mummy's tummy. If we were able to speak and someone asked us what the world was like, we'd describe the small sack we were living in, which represented our world.

We all live inside a box constrained by our consciousness experience, knowledge, beliefs, understanding and imagination etc. Some people's boxes are bigger than others. Pioneering Leaders boxes are bigger; they are the ones pushing the boundaries, going to the leading edge and beyond.

If we were born into the middle of a cardboard box, we'd think the world was like the inside of a cardboard box. Just because we thought the world was like the inside of a cardboard box doesn't mean the world was really like that. Of course, we are not born into a cardboard box; we are probably born into a room somewhere. As far as we are concerned then, the world is the room that we are in. As our life and consciousness unfold, we build knowledge and experience that shapes our view of the world. If we were bought up in a tribal village in a remote Amazonian rainforest, our world would appear like that. If we were brought up in a slum in Calcutta, a major western city, on the African plains or in an Asian paradise, that would shape our view of the world and what we believed was true, real and possible for us.

Imagine all the influences you have had in your life, including from your family, your friends, your teachers, your community leaders, maybe even religious teachers, what you read in the papers, what you hear on the radio, see on TV, learn in the newspapers or what you discover on the internet or social media. We are bought up not just in different countries, but in different cultures, with varying colours of skin and physical attributes to many others. We are the product of all these things combined, and we form judgements about a multitude of different things including what is right and wrong, what is good and bad, what is possible and not possible etc. We are the subject of many rules, traditions and customs in our homes, communities, countries and organisations we may be involved with or influenced by. Most states have standard approaches to things like education, so we learn similar things, have to do similar exams and are judged and judge others in relation to ourselves.

Put all these multitudes of things together, and the picture of different things gets woven into our fabric; they become things that we are certain about. If we take the metaphor or a box, it is like our box has been filled with so much, that seems so real ,that we can quickly feel confident that our understanding of the world reflects the world as it truly is. The certainty makes most people rarely question the fundamental nature of the world and its rules.

The truth is that while our metaphoric box might have expanded considerably; it still exists, we are just not aware of it.

The educational system in many countries favours people who gain the best grades in subjects that are considered academic. The people with the best degrees will frequently go to the Universities that are considered top like, Oxford, Cambridge, Harvard etc. The people who get top degrees from these establishments typically get the top highly paid jobs with the biggest and best employers. They will frequently rise into top positions, getting the best financial rewards, fame and recognition.

Ask most people what the most successful people are like, and they will typically talk about people who are rich and famous, who have lovely houses, cars and luxury five-star lifestyles, top jobs. They are unlikely to describe success as being people who are, healthy happy and fulfilled, doing what they love, with great family and friends who they love and who love them and making a massive positive difference to others.

Pioneering Leaders are usually the ones with the most unconventional outlooks. In 2018 Elon Musk said: "A lot of people don't like humanity and think it is a blight, but I don't. It may sound corny, but love is the answer. Spend more time with your friends and less time on social media." I don't think many high-profile Non-Pioneering Business Leaders would suggest love is the answer. Pioneers like John Lennon and the Dalai Lama would. There is often a philosophical element to Pioneering Leadership, that has a habit of linking to ageless wisdom.

Plato's Cave Allegory – Tapping into Ancient Wisdom

Greek philosopher, Plato who is thought to have lived circa 400BC, creates an allegory, which is a story or metaphor which can be interpreted to obtain meaning.

Plato's "Allegory of the Cave",
drawing by and copyright Markus Maurer

Chapter 4

Imprisonment in the cave

In his allegory of the Cave, Plato describes a cave which is divided into two parts by a wall, which is half the height of the cave. He starts by having Socrates ask Glaucon to imagine a cave where people are imprisoned from birth, and to imagine people chained as prisoners to the wall from birth, such that the cave was all they ever knew. He describes a fire being lit on the far side of the cave on the other side of the wall, furthest away from the people chained to the wall. This fire creates a source of light as well as heat. Directly behind the wall where the people are chained, other people are sent with puppets held up over the wall, which cast shadows, which project onto the wall. These moving shadows are all the prisoners know and are their reality.

Departure from the cave

Plato suggests that if one of the prisoners was released from their chainsPlato suggests that if one of the prisoners was released from their chains and taken to the other side of the wall to see the fire for the first time, it's bright light would most likely blind him, for his eyes have become accustomed to the light on the other side of the wall. If he was told what he was seeing was real, he would not believe it. He would not recognise the puppets, and would not know about reflections, shadows and projections. He would not be able to see clearly, and he would most likely be frightened turn, away from the bright light of the fire and run back to the side of the cave that he knew, which would feel safe and normal, and was where he could see things clearly.

Plato then suggests that the prisoner could be dragged against the will right out of the cave into the real world outside. The brightness of the sunshine would be thousands of times brighter than the light of the fire inside the cave, and even brighter than the part of the cave the prisoner was previously living in. He would be sure to be blinded and dazzled, probably for a very long time until eventually, his eyes would start to accustom themselves to the sunlight. First, all he might be able to see is shadows and outlines, perhaps reflections in water and subsequently the stars and the moonlight and everything in the real world including the sun itself. Only when he can look at the sun directly, can he learn to reason about what it is.

Return to the cave

Plato continues that the prisoner would come to think that the world outside the cave was superior to the world inside the cave. He would feel pity for his fellow prisoners and would want to bring them out into the sunlight too.

He suggests that the returning prisoner would again be temporarily blinded by the relative darkness inside the cave when he returned. The other prisoners would see him temporarily blinded and would think that he had been harmed. They would not want to be dragged outside the cave because they would fear that they too would be blinded, and given a chance, they might even try to kill anyone who tried to drag them out.

Symbolism and Meaning

The allegory contains much symbolism and can be and has been interpreted by different people in different ways. I think a key message is that to all of us, our perception and interpretation about things becomes our reality and our truth, but it doesn't mean to say it is the real truth.

Pioneering Leaders are the ones who've been outside the cave, Non-Pioneering Leaders are the ones inside the cave.

The red pill and blue pill from the film The Matrix

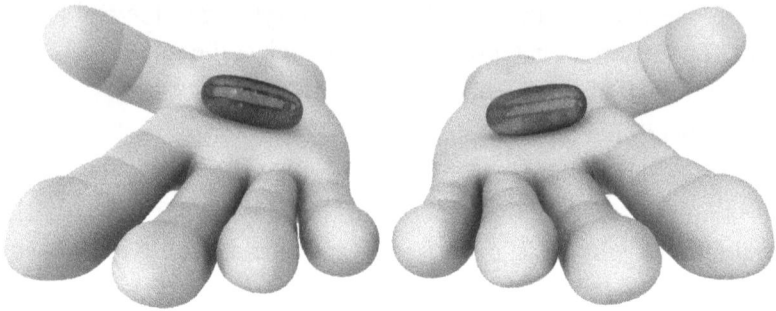

**Blue or Red Pills Enable You to See Different Things:
Illusion or Truth**

"The red pill and its opposite, the blue pill, are a popular cultural meme, a metaphor representing the choice between:

Knowledge, freedom, and the brutal truths of reality (red pill)

Security, happiness and the blissful ignorance of illusion (blue pill)

The terms, popularised in science fiction culture, are derived from the 1999 film The Matrix. In the film, the main character Neo is offered the choice between a red pill and a blue pill by rebel leader Morpheus. The red pill would free him from the enslaving control of the machine-generated dream world and allow him to escape into the real world, but living the "truth of reality" is harsher and more difficult. On the other hand, the blue pill would lead him back to stay in the comfortable simulated reality of the Matrix". Wikipedia

It is possible to make a connection between The Matrix and Plato's Allegory of the Cave. Pioneering Leadership is like taking the red pill, approximately 99% of Non-Pioneering Leaders take the metaphoric blue pill, which means that they see, think, act and know differently to the Pioneering Leaders. Both are in the same world; they just experience different realities and truths.

Neuroscientist David Eagleman explains the human brain

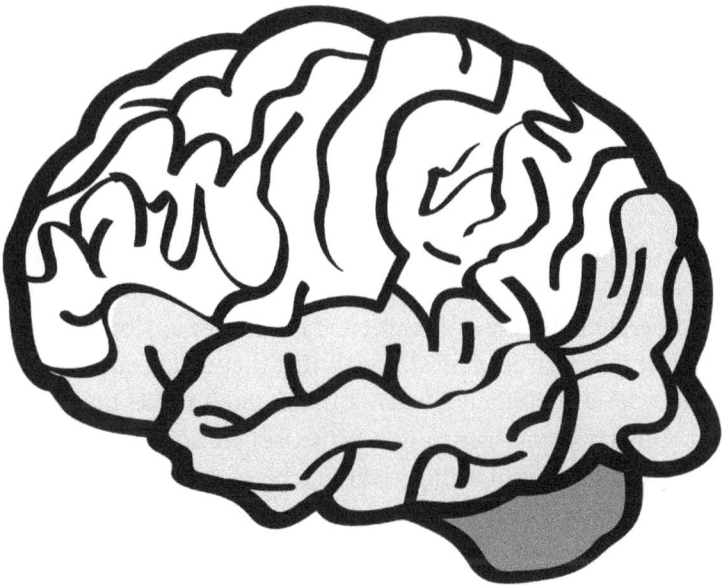

The Human Brain is the Most Complex Thing in the Universe

Chapter 4

David Eagleman is an American neuroscientist writer and documentary filmmaker who teaches at Stanford University as an adjunct professor in the Department of Psychiatry & Behavioural Sciences.

He made a fantastic six-part documentary series which explained that the human brain is the most complicated thing in the universe, revealing fascinating facts in the six episodes that can change the way you see yourself and the world:

1. What Is Reality?

2. What Makes Me Me?

3. Who's in Control?

4. How Do I Decide?

5. Why Do I Need You?

6. Who Will We Be?

Our brains are like supercomputers and hard drives that remain hidden away encapsulated in our skulls and tissue. Unless we have a brain operation, they are never seen, it is like they are locked in a dark room, yet the electrochemical signals that they send and receive, provide us with a functioning body, a mind and a perception of reality that seems vivid and true to us. Our senses are so realistic, they give us certainty, but they don't necessarily represent the actual truth. It is possible that other animals would see the world in very different ways to the way we see it.

Psychology teaches us that we see the world as we are not as it indeed is

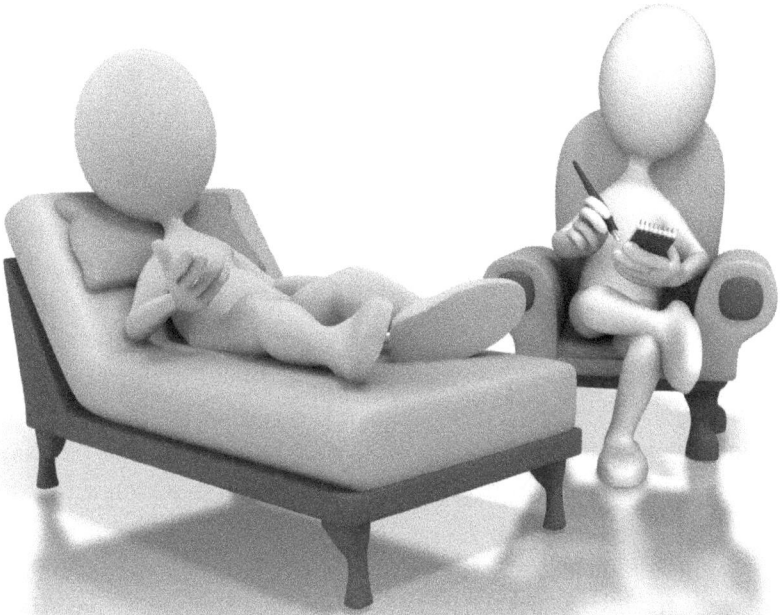

Psychology can be very revealing

In the early 1990's I was leading a technology company that was struggling in a market that had stalled following a period of immense growth. I was the metaphoric captain of the ship, responsible for the company and as such I felt a huge responsibility. When things are not going well, people often look to blame the captain, and as the captain, the first place that I looked to, to turn around the situation was myself.

A good friend introduced me to a coach who was a specialist in psychometric profiling tools. It provided an epiphany when I discovered psychology and learnt that two people could see or experience the same thing yet see and experience something completely different. I found that we all see the world, not as it really is, but as we are; it is not logical, it is psychological. I was so amazed by what I discovered that I studied and became certified on a leading psychometric assessment tool. I subsequently embarked on a further study to identify and understand other psychometric and other assessment tools.

You might be familiar with the phrase "one man's terrorist is another man's freedom fighter". This is one example where different people see the same thing through different lenses. Pioneering Leaders and Non-Pioneering Leaders can see the same thing yet perceive it and understand it in entirely different ways. Ex-South African President, Nelson Mandela, was once the head of the armed wing of the African National Congress (ANC), was imprisoned for 27 years and subsequently became the President of South Africa, receiving numerous awards including the Nobel Peace Prize in 1993. He was on the USA's terrorist watch list until 2008.

Natural Pioneering Leaders can be identified belonging to certain psychological types, but what they do can be learnt and practised by anyone with the motivation and desire who is prepared to put in the effort required.

The truth and illusion

The Truth and Illusion are Sometimes Hard to Separate

Humanity has long grappled with a desire to know the truth about things, yet appears continually challenged by illusion, misunderstanding, false and conflicting beliefs and evidence. Science often seems at odds with religion, philosophy and ancient wisdom.

We like to value and trust science, but history is littered with widely accepted scientific facts that subsequently turned out to be wrong. Even the greatest minds and most intelligent people are capable of being wrong. Scientific theories can remain valid until they are disproved. Even Einstein changed his mind on things like "Einstein's Static Universe", where he changed his mind, abandoning his static model of the universe and proposed an expanding model.

Chapter 4

As human beings, we crave for the truth; we are desperate for knowledge, we value it, even worship it and make it central to our existence. Our educational systems are based on acquiring knowledge, we are frequently tested on our ability to retain and understand it, yet we are rarely taught to question it, challenge it, use our imagination and come up with new ideas.

Collectively we struggle to know even basic things like what is right or wrong and good or bad. Sometimes we can be confused, how often are we told something is good for us, subsequently to be told it is not. I remember when diesel cars were considered to be good for the environment because they were more fuel efficient than petrol (gasoline) cars, yet now the experts tell us that they are not, because the pollution caused by using diesel fuel is more harmful than that caused by using petrol. Plastic was once held up to be a wonder material, but now we have discovered it presents one of the greatest threats to the environment.

We are always looking for someone to follow, someone who has wisdom and knows more than us.

We are always looking for someone to follow, who has wisdom and knows more than us. In the absence of an expert or great leader we trust, we will often look to see what others are doing or believing that are around us, and then do or believe the same. At least that way, if we are wrong, we are wrong with everyone else, and that seems to us much better than being the only person that is wrong. It takes a strong person to stand alone, to go against the grain, to dare to be different even if you have certainty that you are right. Often you don't have certainty, you just have a hunch, and to discover if that hunch is right, can often require immense courage.

We are all capable of being manipulated and controlled by others, from childhood, through to adulthood. There are always plenty of people who have power and control over us, from world leaders downwards.

The simple fact is that truth matters, and illusion is our biggest foe. Few people really recognise that fact, but Pioneering Leaders do, and dealing with those issues is central to their existence.

Optical Illusion

Sometimes things look different when you look deeper

I have always been fascinated by magicians, who appear to do unbelievable things, that you see with your own eyes. Sometimes the only explanation we can come up with to explain what magicians have done, is to believe that it was true magic, yet we know that most, if not all magic that we see, is merely a clever illusion or trick. I am intrigued to see videos that explain how magic tricks are done. How can you saw someone in half and then put them back together again? I love it when Penn & Teller explain how tricks are done.

Our eyes can and do deceive us more often than we recognise. Every now and again we get to see it, like the dress story that went viral where different people seeing the same dress could see it as either white and gold or blue and black. These colours are so vastly different, you wouldn't think it is possible, but it is. There are so many optical illusions, none of us should trust what we see entirely.

Audio Illusion

Laurel or Yanny?

We are also capable of being tricked by our ears too. There are plenty of audio illusions too. In 2018 an audio illusion went viral where an audio was recognised clearly by some people as "Laurel" and by others as "Yanny". We shouldn't believe all that we hear also.

The majority isn't always right

"Whenever you find yourself on the side of the majority, it is time to pause and reflect." Mark Twain

"Wrong does not cease to be wrong because the majority share in it." Tolstoy

"When you're the only sane person, you look like the only insane person." "I never feel unsafe except for when the majority is on my side." Poet Criss Jami (Christopher James Gilbert)

"In matters of conscience, the law of the majority has no place." Mahatma Gandhi

Just because the majority of people believe something, doesn't mean that they are right, yet we often gain colossal reassurance and reinforcement of our beliefs if the majority hold the same views that we do, especially if the majority comprises people with apparently impeccable credentials like Nobel Laureates or people who have significant authority.

In the time leading up to the financial crisis of 2007 / 2008, most senior people in the financial industry, commentators, experts, academics, politicians, journalists, economists, central bankers and world leaders, didn't seem to think that we are on the edge of a financial calamity.

Multi-billionaire and one of the world's most successful ever investor, Warren Buffett once said that as an investor, it is wise to be "fearful when others are greedy, and greedy when others are fearful."

Chapter 4

While the majority are not always right, they are also not always wrong. It is much harder to take a minority position in any situation, it requires courage and belief, which is even more challenging to find, when you may well also have great uncertainty and doubt. By definition Pioneering Leaders are pioneering, challenging the status quo/business and usual and the path of the majority. They are the ones who are changing the game, breaking the mould, disrupting and blazing new trails. Pioneering Leaders are the people who drive progress, gain advantage and lead the way for others to follow.

We often assume that in an argument that one party is right and the other is wrong. We rarely consider the possibility that both can be right or that things might be finely balanced, or that factors not considered or perhaps even known could impact who was right and how was wrong.

Pioneering Leaders are more likely to recognise all points of view, even if they settle for positions different to the majority.

There is nearly always the possibility of a better way or something better

The bar is always being raised

At every Olympic Games, someone breaks a new record, runs faster, jumps further or higher; you wouldn't think it was possible. There is always the possibility of discovering better ways, creating better things and bringing new things into existence. The industrial revolution, through to the modern technological age has seen greater advances and inventions occurring at a greater speed than at any previous time in human history. Pioneering Leadership is the thing that is responsible for these things, which makes it the most important, relevant and powerful strategy available to humanity.

"To some the box is a safe haven, to others it is a prison. Outside the box is unlimited possibility, potential and opportunity."

Chapter 5

Pioneering Leadership in Uncharted Waters Framework Introduction

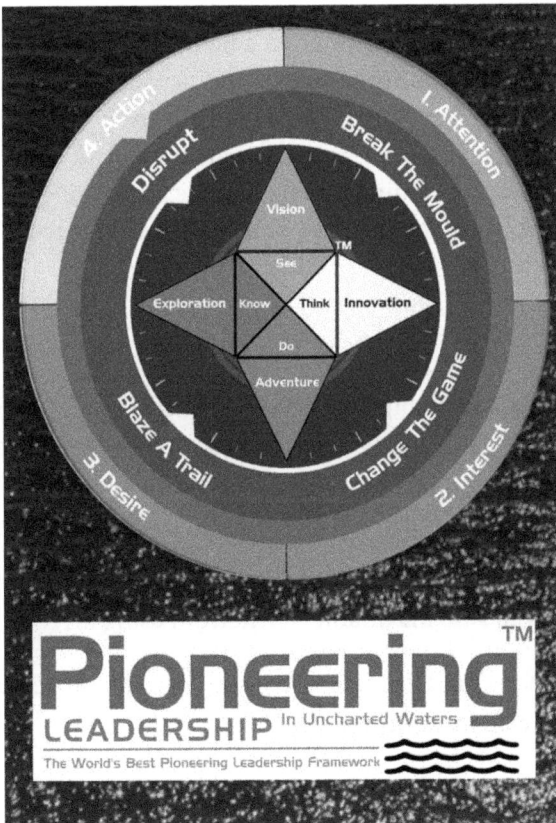

Chapter 5

Introduction to the Pioneering Leadership in Uncharted Waters™

Ownership of the term "Pioneering Leadership."

I don't own the term "Pioneering Leadership", although I do own the domain www.PioneeringLeadership.com. I accept that it can mean different things to different people and that others have already written about it. This book reflects my personal views; I want to make clear that my views may or may not be correct, you can decide that.

Unique Definition of Pioneering Leadership to Avoid Confusion

To avoid confusion, I have given a name to my views, knowledge, ideas and solution relating to Pioneering Leadership, which you can use if you need to talk to others about it, that name is "Pioneering Leadership in Uncharted Waters™", which is my trademark and intellectual property. For ease of reading, throughout the book, I refer to "Pioneering Leadership", not "Pioneering Leadership in Uncharted Waters".

Purpose of Pioneering Leadership in Uncharted Waters Framework

Pioneering Leadership in Uncharted Waters Framework was created to facilitate four primary things relating to Pioneering Leadership:

1. Understanding.

2. How to use It.

3. How to gain maximum benefit from using It.

4. A shared understanding so people can work together to use it and achieve benefits.

Pioneering Leadership Doesn't Have to Involve Leading Others

Pioneering Leadership doesn't have to involve leading others, a business, other types of organisation, a community, a country or a cause; it could include leading yourself and leading by being in front of others or competing against others like a sports person.

If Pioneering Leadership is The Most Powerful Strategy on Earth – Why Isn't That Widely Known?

Pioneering Leadership is not very well understood; in many respects, it is simple to understand, but when you dig a bit deeper, you will discover nuances and different ways of seeing it, that can change everything. I've boldly stated that "Pioneering Leadership is the most powerful strategy available to mankind" and I believe that to be a 100% accurate statement. You might be thinking, if this is the case, why aren't I already aware of that, in fact, why aren't most other people aware of it too, and why isn't it taught at schools, universities, colleges, business schools and in homes around the world as a subject of the utmost significance and highest importance? I think it should be, and with this book and the Pioneering Leadership Academy that I have established, I hope will help to rectify the deficit in Pioneering Leadership Training.

Pioneering Leadership and Power

Rightly or wrongly, Pioneering Leadership is tied up with power. Often those in or with power don't want to empower those not in power or with power; to them, increasing people having access to and using the immense power of Pioneering Leadership, represents perhaps the most significant threat, since the power of Pioneering Leadership comes from differential, i.e. difference with others. The levers and instruments of power, potential, possibility and opportunity are esoteric; closely guarded secrets, known by the few, or perhaps more accurately not shared. You would have thought that discovering a hugely powerful secret that could change everything, would itself be the game changer, but surprisingly it isn't. Unless you change and leverage the power inherent in the mysteries of Pioneering Leadership, nothing changes. Doctors know more than average people what you need to do to live a healthy lifestyle and the consequences of not doing so, yet many doctors don't use the knowledge they have to be healthy themselves. It is not what you know; it is what you do that usually matters most.

Many factors can and most probably will, prevent you from using Pioneering Leadership like fear, desire to conform to normality, peer pressure, conditioning etc. The Pioneering Leadership in Uncharted Waters Framework will help you to recognise them, overcome them and learn what you have to do, even if that is getting someone else to do Pioneering Leadership for you.

Pioneering Leadership in Uncharted Waters Framework - Background

I can't believe how long it took me to create the Pioneering Leadership in Uncharted Waters Framework; I think it is because while the essence of Pioneering Leadership is simple, implementing it and fully understanding it isn't. I wanted to share the power of Pioneering Leadership to help more people to create better futures and solve difficult problems and challenges, and I thought the best way of doing that was to make it as high level, simple and transparent as possible.

I've created a more detailed framework that forms the basis for the "Pioneering Leadership in Uncharted Waters Program", which has been designed to support Senior Leaders and Organisations who are serious about using Pioneering Leadership and want to take it to a deeper level. To find out more visit www.PioneeringLeadership.com.

Pioneering Leadership has been central to my life for almost as long as I can remember. I've spent years discovering it, exploring it, learning it, meeting highly successful Pioneering Leaders and using it. As a Natural (Born) Pioneering Leader, Pioneering Leadership comes naturally to me and is an integral part of my personality and identity. It has taken years of self-discovery and the use of multiple assessments tools to figure this out. I scored as an "Extreme Game Changer" on the GC Index, and on the Jungian psychology-based Insights Deeper Discovery assessment, my number one archetype out of 72 possible ones, was "Pioneer". Pretty much every assessment tool I have used points strongly to Pioneering, and the attributes needed for Pioneering. The bottom line is that Pioneering is undoubtedly my thing, and I am passionate and enthusiastic about what it offers, to create a better future. If I am honest, being a natural Pioneering Leader seems like a mixed blessing, because I've always felt different in some way, the odd one out. The counter side to that is the achievement of some extraordinary things. I think society is terrible as cultivating non-artistic creativity. The Pioneering Leadership in Uncharted Waters Framework is simple enough that most people should be able to understand how to use it to unlock immense creative value. My biggest desire is to make a positive difference in the world and help others to use Pioneering Leadership to solve the most significant and most important problems and to create and exploit the most incredible and worthwhile opportunities.

According to PWC, 3% of jobs are at risk of automation in the early 2020's, but 30% are at risk by the mid-2030's. Artificial Intelligence and automation is going to have a profound impact on careers, lives and the world, and there will be winners and losers. Non-Pioneering Leaders, doing same or similar things to other people will be at much higher risk of having their jobs automated than Pioneering Leaders. Computers will struggle to compete with the imagination, creativity and pioneering spirit of human beings. It will be the Pioneering Leaders who have the imagination, vision and resourcefulness to create the new world. Ponder on that, when thinking about whether to dismiss or ignore Pioneering Leadership.

Chapter 5

The Game – Primarily Non-Arts Based Creativity

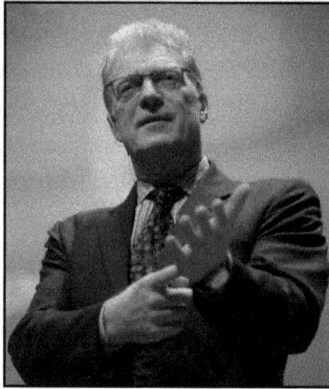

(© Sebastiaan ter Burg)

"We are educating people out of their creativity."
Educationalist, Sir Ken Robinson

Professor, Sir Ken Robinson, delivered the most-watched TED Talk of all time: "Do Schools Kill Creativity", which has been viewed over 50 million times. "He champions a radical rethink of our school systems, to cultivate creativity and acknowledge multiple types of intelligence. We've been educated to become good workers, rather than creative thinkers. Students with restless minds and bodies -- far from being cultivated for their energy and curiosity -- are ignored or even stigmatised, with terrible consequences. We are educating people out of their creativity." TED.com I agree with him.

Pioneering Leadership is at its heart "creativity turned into outcomes and results". When we think about Creativity and the Creative Industries, we typically think of Art and Design and things like Writing, Photography, Film Making, Theatre, Music, Dance, Drama etc.

I couldn't have been prouder than when my eldest daughter Kezia, graduated from Arts University Bournemouth with a First-Class

Honours Degree (Fine Art Photography). At the graduation ceremony, the University Chancellor discussed the vast economic significance of the Creative Sector, and how often it is undervalued. "The £92 billion UK creative industries is growing at a faster rate than the whole of the UK economy, and accounts for 1 in 11 jobs". I couldn't help but think how crucial Pioneering Leadership was to the world and every field of human endeavour, yet it doesn't appear on syllabuses at schools, there are no university courses on it to the best of my knowledge, yet it is arguably the most powerful and important strategy in the world. I once started but didn't complete a master's degree in Business Innovation and Creativity, and I notice there are still a handful of similar courses still in existence. Pioneering Leadership doesn't appear on most syllabuses even in this niche field.

Pioneering Leadership is Non-Arts Based Creativity

Non-Arts based creativity, e.g. things not taught at universities like Arts University Bournemouth is still at the margins, yet its impact in the world is the most profound of all. Pioneering Leadership is the pinnacle of non-arts-based creativity. Sir Ken Robinson talks about how he believes schools are "educating people out of their creativity". I hope the Pioneering Leadership Academy and the Pioneering Leadership in Uncharted Waters Framework, can help to educate people back into their non-arts-based creativity. There are good reasons why this isn't just desirable, it is essential because the world is facing multiple existential threats and Pioneering Leadership offers the best solutions. We are living in a time when we are on a knife-edge between huge threats and massive opportunities, economically, politically, socially, environmentally and at organisation and individual levels. Pioneering Leadership has never been more relevant or more important.

Take a Holiday – Change Your Environment – Go on Real Life Adventure

When I left school, my first job was as a Royal Naval Officer. On my first day, I arrived at Britannia Royal Naval College in Dartmouth, which is where the Queen first met Prince Philip and immediately started a process called "militarisation". As I am sure you can imagine, the military has a unique way of operating, that differs from the civilian way. Immediately your civilian clothes are replaced by military uniforms, if you didn't arrive with a military haircut, you are soon given one, and before long, you are sharply inducted into the military way of life. Timekeeping is paramount; if you are not five minutes early, you are late. You need to be at the right place at the right time, with the right uniform and the right equipment, all to the right standard. Boots and shoes need to be polished to a high gloss, creases in your trousers need to be perfect, and your hygiene needs to be perfect. Your bed had to be made in a particular way, and your clothes stored in drawers had to be laid out in a set way. Even your dirty clothes in your dirty clothes basket had to be folded in a special way and were inspected. Everything was inspected all the time; a tiny variation was a massive offence. At times like preceding important inspections, we'd sleep on the floor, to keep our beds perfect. Before long, we were learning to march on the parade ground, line up for inspections and present ourselves. All this happened with exceedingly long working days, extreme fitness regime and intense naval studies. If you've ever seen the film "An Officer and a Gentleman", starring Richard Gere, you'll see the dramatisation the US Navy equivalent of Naval Officer Training. While the Royal Navy is different, there are similarities.

It is amazing how quickly the transition is from civilian life to military life, but the difference is enormous. Within a relatively short time, you are in many ways a different person with a different outlook; you are capable of being put in life-threatening situations and functioning with professionalism. Not that long after joining, I was on a ship at sea in a hurricane, with steady 120 mph winds and mountainous seas.

If you are not a natural Pioneering Leader, you need to find a way of disconnecting/detaching from your current mindset and modus operandi, and open yourself to seeing things, thinking and acting in new ways. The best way of doing this is to find a way of temporary changing:

1. Your environment.

2. The people you are with perhaps.

3. Developing your Pioneering Leadership skills.

You might be pleased to know, that you don't need to go to a military type boot camp. Instead you can take a holiday somewhere inspiring, go on a real-life adventure, perhaps a yachting trip into metaphoric uncharted waters or climb a mountain or walk and camp in a wilderness somewhere. It can do wonders for clearing your mind of the old and allowing inspiration and the new to come in. Inspiration is an essential part of Pioneering Leadership, anything that inspires you and is different from normal is good.

Just before finishing this book, I took two weeks yachting around Mallorca and Menorca. Taking a break from your usual day to day things, connecting with the natural world is a perfect way of preparing for Pioneering Leadership. The more adventurous, challenging and different the better. Doing this isn't essential, but it can help, inspire you and make you see things differently and reconsider what might be possible.

What you need to search for, is an inner trigger that changes something inside you, perhaps something that connects you to a higher purpose and higher ideals. Transitioning towards Pioneering Leadership can mean ditching people who pull you down, hold you back or get in your way. You are best connecting with positive can-do people, who are open to new possibilities.

Open Your Mind

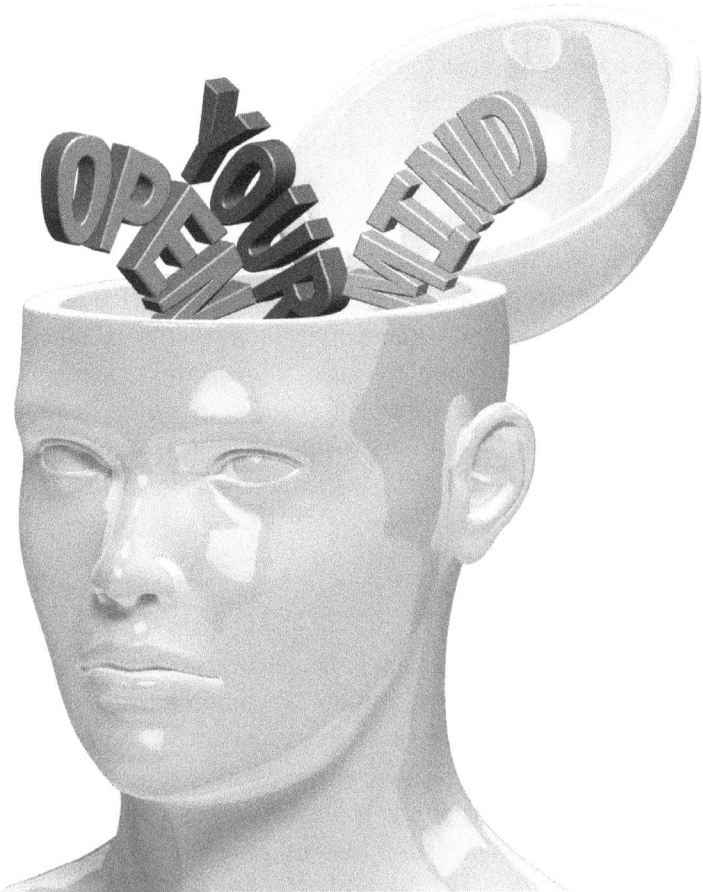

Open Your Mind to New Possibilities and Opportunities

Suggesting anyone is closed minded, is a big insult. If someone suggests we are closed-minded, it hurts, we are likely to get defensive and deny it; this is human nature. Instinctively we all like to think we are open-minded, but what we think and what we truly are, is often very different. One of the most powerful lessons I ever learnt was psychology, and it is that we see the world not as it truly is, but as we are. In Chapter 4, I discussed perceptions, which describes this very issue.

Unless you can open your mind to possibility, potential and opportunity, you won't be able to practice Pioneering Leadership. The more you can open your mind to these things, the more successful you are likely to be.

We all can be selective in which situations we are open-minded and which we are not, but generally speaking, because Natural Pioneering Leaders are those most open for change, transformation and something new, they tend to be the ones with the most open minds. Their Achilles heel, however, can be the risk of falling in love with their ideas so much, that they become unwilling to listen to others whose opinions can be valid and valuable. Sometimes Pioneering Leaders need to be grounded and brought down to earth, yet there is a fine line between doing this and destroying the value that they can deliver. Pioneering Leaders are excellent at seeing things that Non-Pioneering Leaders don't.

Make Connections

Neurologist, Paul Howard-Jones uncovers what happens in our heads when we are creating and how the brain impacts our creativity. He suggests that we are generally more creative and come up with ideas best when we are relaxed, where we have time and space to let our minds drift. It is helpful to challenge people to make connections between pieces of information that are generally not associated. The key barriers to creativity is becoming fixated on things, that happens the more familiar we get with things. Teamwork can make you more creative. The foundation for civilisations happened when communication started between well-connected populations. Neuroscience can explain what is going on in our brains when Pioneering Leadership is practised.

Join the Dots

Pioneering Leadership involves metaphorically joining the dots and making the connections that Paul Howard-Jones, suggested are so important.

Tune in to the Benefits

Pioneering Leadership can seem abstract and irrelevant if you don't give it context and don't relate it to your situation. You need to unlock the power of Pioneering Leadership by thinking about what it can do for you, versus the strategies you are currently using.

It is useful if you can have an "Ah Ha Moment", where you awake to the possibility, potential and opportunities that it offers you. Once you unlock it, it is like letting the genie out the bottle, you can never put it back in. Recognising it and tuning in to it is like an epiphany and happens when and if you can increase your consciousness of it.

If you manage to tune into it, your life will never be quite the same again. Try to reach a point where you are so connected to the benefits, they become real for you, where you expect the outcomes, and feel them, and get excited by them before you've achieved them.

Imagine Pioneering Leadership as something valuable that belongs to you, but is hidden away in a safe, all you've got to be able to do is to find a way of unlocking it. Fortunately, you don't need to be a locksmith, you just need to use the Pioneering Leadership in Uncharted Waters Framework diligently.

Learn to Love New Things

Learn to love new things:
1. New thinking.
2. New ideas.
3. New solutions.
4. New ways.

Unlock the Most Powerful Strategy on Earth

Make	1. Make the seemingly impossible possible.
Solve	2. Solve difficult problems or challenges in unique ways.
Create & exploit	3. Create and exploit exciting opportunities.
Compete	4. Compete against tough competition and win.
Achieve	5. Achieve extraordinary things.
Drive and Move	6. Drive progress and move the human race forwards.

Pioneering Leadership is Virtually Everywhere

You'll Find Pioneering Leadership Almost Everywhere

Pioneering Leadership is not new; in fact, it has probably been around for a long as modern man, (Homo Sapiens) have been around.

It is likely being used all around you, and will already be impacting many things in your life; you may even be using it yourself. It is just that you may not see it, and may not be aware of it, and probably don't use "Pioneering Leadership as a label for it. It is like oxygen; you know that it is in the air that you breathe, but you don't often think about the miracle of how it enables you to live. Think of Pioneering Leadership as an umbrella that covers many things that you might be very familiar with and also things you don't know about. You might be familiar with concepts, like innovation and creativity, yet not all innovation and creativity is Pioneering. You might have heard of concepts like Disruptive Innovation and Blue Ocean Strategy, both the topic of books that have sold millions of copies and are taught in top business schools and used by many people around the world. These are examples of Pioneering Leadership strategies put into action, but Pioneering Leadership is bigger than these things, and more than these things, because it encompasses the whole, not just the part that these examples represent.

Consider the fact that just because you perhaps don't see and recognise Pioneering Leadership in action in the world, doesn't mean it doesn't exist; you can see its results everywhere in medicine, science, business, engineering, the military, sport and in virtually every type of human endeavour. There are plenty of things in the world that you don't necessarily see or are not consciously aware of like radio waves and the laws of nature. When you are aware of these things, you can believe in them and see evidence of their presence, and even learn how to harness them for your benefit. Pioneering Leadership is like that, to use it, you have to be able to recognise it and understand it, and then learn how to harness its power for your benefit. It can often start off being hard to use, but like anything becomes easier with practice and experience.

The Concepts Behind the Pioneering Leadership in Uncharted Waters Framework

At the Core of The Pioneering Leadership Framework is the concept that at the highest level, there are just two generic strategies, which apply to just about every human endeavour or enterprise. These two strategies are:

1.   Non-Pioneering Leadership (used by approx. 99% of people 99% of the time).

2.   Pioneering Leadership (used by approximately 1% of people).

The Framework stems from the familiar metaphor which has three variants:

1.   Thinking Outside the Box.

2.   Thinking Out the Box.

3.   Thinking Outside the Square.

Pioneering Leadership is about more than just thinking outside the box or square, but the term is widely understood to represent thinking differently, unconventionally, or from a new perspective and often refers to novel or creative thinking, new paradigms etc.

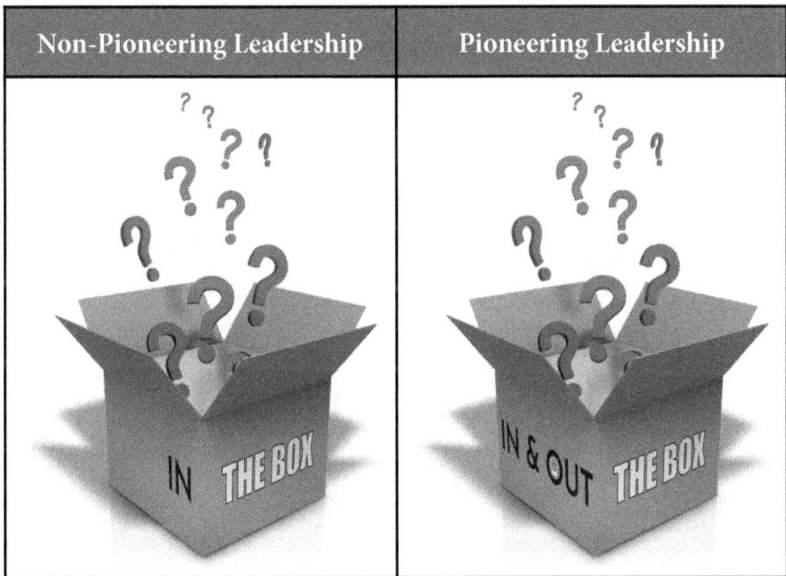

Non-Pioneering Leadership	Pioneering Leadership

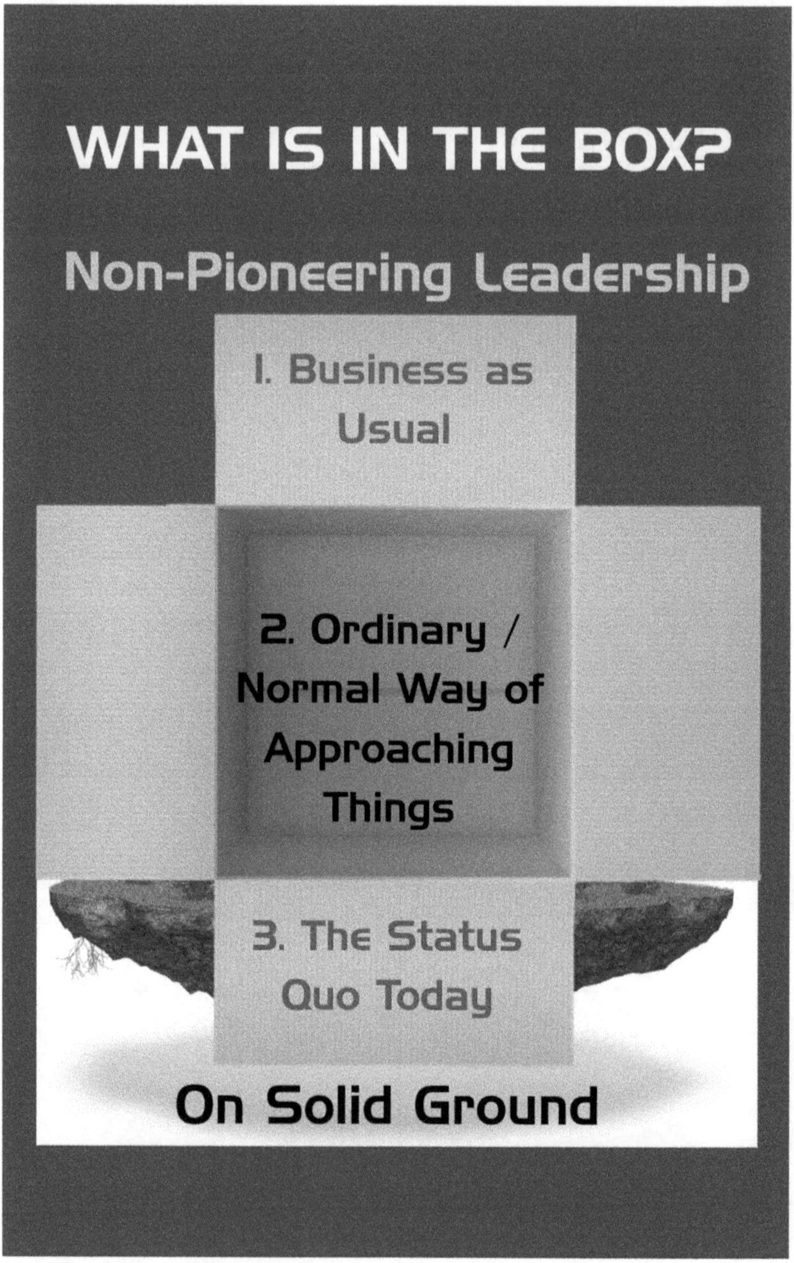

WHAT IS IN THE BOX?

Non-Pioneering Leadership

1. Business as Usual

2. Ordinary / Normal Way of Approaching Things

3. The Status Quo Today

On Solid Ground

WHAT IS OUT THE BOX?

Pioneering Leadership

1. Opposite of Business as Usual
2. Extraordinary Approach
3. Pursuit of New, Different & Better

OUTSIDE The BOX

Uncharted Waters

Non-Pioneering Leadership represents the status quo and the mainstream 99%. Pioneering Leadership represents the 1% and doesn't just reflect the out the box thinking; it is greedier than that; it reflects both in and out the box thinking and more.

In the Box	In and Out the Box
Non-Pioneering Leadership	Pioneering Leadership

Based on "Solid Ground"	Involves Venturing Into Uncharted Waters
Predominantly Based on "The Known" Which is Finite **"Knowledge"**	Based on "The Known and The Unknown" Which is Infinite **"Knowledge and Unlimited Imagination"**
Knowledge Represents A Part	Knowledge + Unlimited Imagination Represents The Whole "The Whole is Always Greater Than A Part"

"Imagination is more important than knowledge. For knowledge is limited, whereas imagination embraces the entire world, stimulating progress, giving birth to evolution". Albert Einstein

Out The Box – Framework Core

While Pioneering Leadership in the Pioneering Leadership in Uncharted Waters Framework stems from the metaphor of "Thinking Outside the Box", it is much more than this, and more than a metaphor.

Non-Pioneering Leadership is "in the box", and Pioneering Leadership is "in and out of the box".

In the Pioneering Leadership in Uncharted Waters Framework "The Box" has a specific definition, which defines each of the four sides of the box; this will be explained later. Having established what the box is, the Framework Provides a means to get outside the box to achieve better accomplishments, outcomes, results and success and a better future, which is the core of Pioneering Leadership.

Pioneering Leadership is about driving progress, doing what has not been done before, or doing things in new creative ways or bringing into existence something that doesn't currently exist. It is the opposite of business as usual and can be recognised with the four metaphors: Changing the Game, Breaking the Mould, Blazing a Trail and Disrupting.

"Strive to be first, new, different and better"

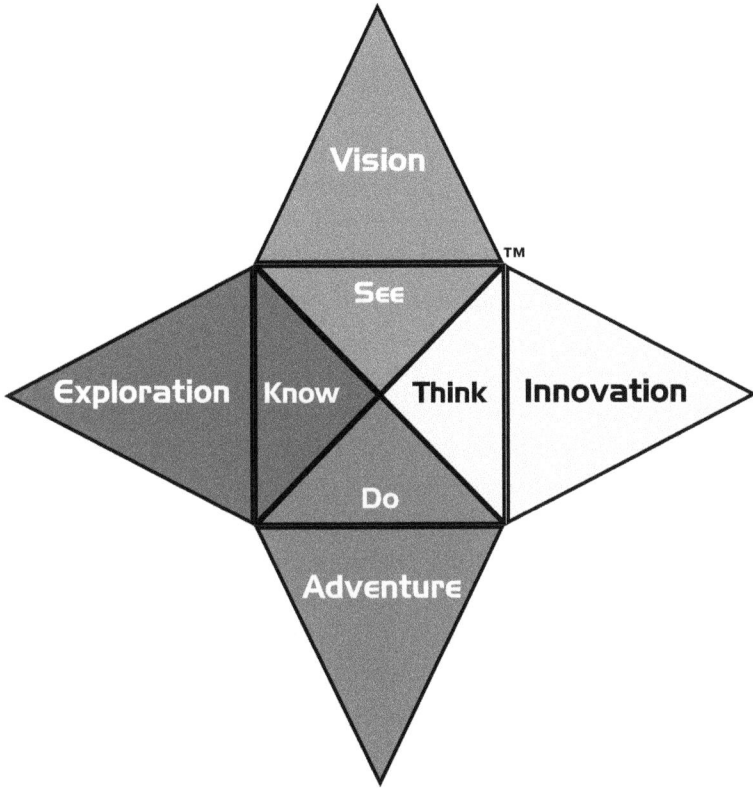

Pioneering Leadership in Uncharted Waters Framework Core is Build Around a Box

The Pioneering Leadership in Uncharted Waters Framework Core, is a star shape that is built around a square box. The points of the star point away from the box at the centre, and each point of the star points to one element of what you need to do to get out of the box. It is challenging to think about endeavours generally when you spend most of your life thinking about specific tasks and objectives you need to achieve.

Chapter 5

Framework Deeper Understanding

When learning anything new, one expects to be able to follow a sequence of steps that take you from where you are now to where you want to be. Pioneering Leadership offers many chicken and egg scenarios, where you must consider which comes first. Pioneering Leadership can take you from A to B like a project plan, but it offers an open agenda with infinite possibilities. With Pioneering Leadership you might start with an outcome and try and turn it into an objective. An example of this could be the legendary story of 3M's Post-It Note, where a scientist reportedly was trying to develop a super-strong adhesive but instead accidentally created a "low-tack," reusable, pressure-sensitive adhesive. For five years it was a solution without a problem or application. Eventually almost every office in the world ended up having Post It notes. While the inventor Alan Amron eventually won a lawsuit against 3M regarding the technology used, the story about a solution without a problem appears to be true and provides a useful example for how Pioneering Leadership doesn't have to start with a known objective. Scientists using Pioneering Leadership with curiosity, ask questions and make investigations develop hypotheses and make discoveries, that create unimaginable possibilities. Sometimes the starting point is an idea, a thought or an observation, or sometimes an adventure is a catalyst or discovery of an unintended consequence or a connection that hadn't previously been known.

The Framework uses four metaphors for getting outside the box, which are:

1. Breaking the mould.

2. Changing the game.

3. Blazing a trail.

4. Disrupting.

Other metaphors however are possible.

At the heart of Pioneering Leadership is the concept of "Cause and Effect", which has just three elements that all begin with the letter "O" -"The Three O's":

1. Objective – What do you want?

2. Option – What options are there to get what you want?

3. Outcome – What results can you get from the options used?

The Objective and Outcomes are obvious. The Option is how the outcome is achieved or what action is carried out to create either an objective or an outcome.

Pioneering Leaders work with objectives, options and outcomes to create a better future.

Pioneering Leadership in Uncharted Waters Framework offers four interdependent elements to work with to break out the box, break the mould, change the game, blaze a trail and disrupt. These are:

1. Vision

2. Innovation

3. Adventure

4. Exploration

You should think of Pioneering Leadership as a high-level strategy you can use to achieve extraordinary outcomes.

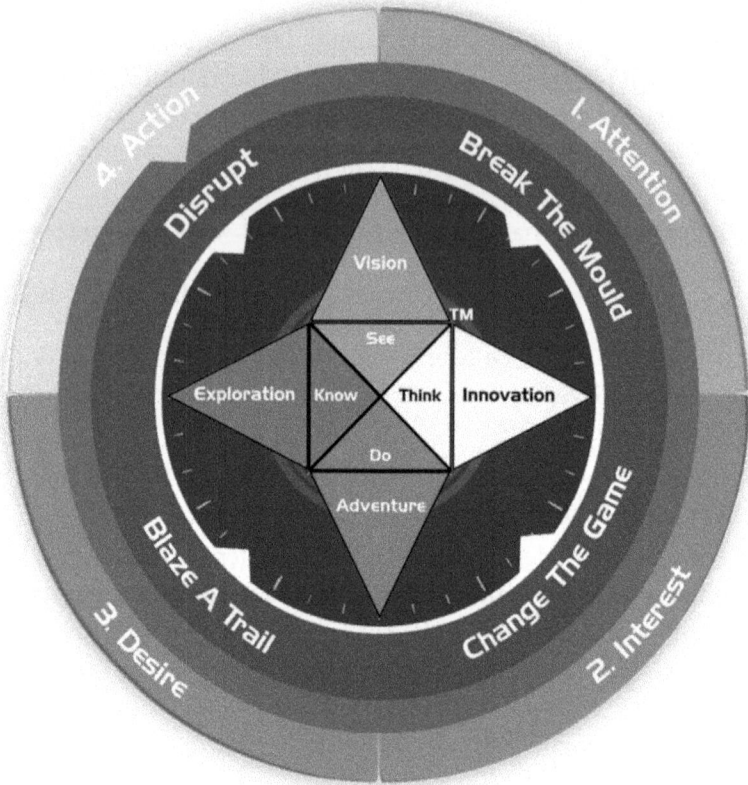

"Start at The Outside and Move Inwards"

The High-Level Pioneering Leadership in Uncharted Waters Framework

With tremendous forces stacked against you using Pioneering Leadership, you are much more likely to find yourself with the 99% using Non-Pioneering Leadership in whatever you are doing. Non-Pioneering Leadership is often the best strategy.

Salesman and Marketers have long understood and been able to work with human nature, sufficiently to understand what it takes for people to buy into anything. This knowledge can help you to buy into

Pioneering Leadership. Unless you are a Natural (Born) Pioneering Leader, you are likely to have to buy into Pioneering Leadership as a concept, to stand any chance of using it. To buy into it, you've first got be aware that it exists and to find a reason to think about it and bring it to your top of mind awareness. You've then got to get interested in it, and discover what it can offer you. There then has to be a desire in you to want to use it, and that desire has got to be strong enough to make you take action and attempt to use it. To get to the start line where you use Pioneering Leadership, you, therefore, need to get through the following stages:

1. Attention.

2. Interest.

3. Desire.

4. Action.

Orientation Towards Pioneering Leadership

The four metaphors of Pioneering Leadership are designed to orientate you towards Pioneering. It is the opposite of business as usual, the ordinary and conventional.

The metaphors evoke the essence of Pioneering Leadership.

- Break the Mould

- Change the Game

- Blaze a Trail

- Disrupt

Think about being, new, different and better.

Chapter 5

The 4 Stages of Competence

The question what is Pioneering Leadership seems like it should be easy to answer, ut isn't. Pioneering Leadership is a skill that can be learnt. It, therefore, shares generic stages of competence applicable when learning anything new. You can't expect instant mastery, although immediate results are possible. Pioneering Leadership is as suited to someone who is in for the long haul of extraordinary effort to achieve exceptional results, as it is for someone who wants a shortcut to the best results without the remarkable effort that others put in. Pioneering Leadership can be used for small everyday things, as well as for solving the most complex problems facing humanity.

Some people will slave away on career paths to achieve the best results, where others will use Pioneering Leadership to adopt a four hour work week, earning considerably more for less effort, with greater enjoyment.

You may or may not get instant extraordinary results with Pioneering Leadership, but it is always possible to improve your Pioneering Leadership Skills. The more proficient you are at Pioneering Leadership, the better the likely results you will achieve.

Have an awareness of where you are on the stages of competence framework and remember the possibility for improvement is never ending.

Pioneering™
LEADERSHIP In Uncharted Waters
The World's Best Pioneering Leadership Framework

4 Pioneering Leadership Stages

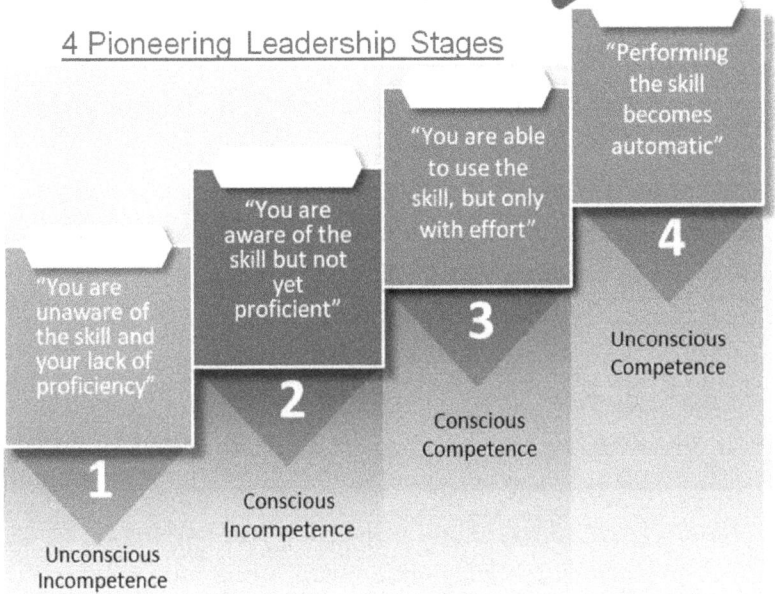

"You are unaware of the skill and your lack of proficiency"

1
Unconscious Incompetence

"You are aware of the skill but not yet proficient"

2
Conscious Incompetence

"You are able to use the skill, but only with effort"

3
Conscious Competence

"Performing the skill becomes automatic"

4
Unconscious Competence

According to Wikipedia, Martin M. Broadwell created a "Four Stages of Competence" framework in 1969, which later became known as "Four Stages for Learning Any New Skill". This is often wrongly attributed to Abraham Maslow who was the creator of Maslow's Hierarchy of Human Needs. It might help you to position yourself on this framework when learning to practice Pioneering Leadership so that you can see from a broad perspective what you need to achieve.

The question "what is Pioneering Leadership", seems like it should be easy to answer, but in reality, it is not. Understanding its usefulness to you and being able to use it, requires a reasonable level of understanding. It is easy to understand a part of what it is, but it is much more difficult to understand the whole of what it is. It is easy to misunderstand it and think you know what it is, but trying to deliver a short, simple explanation in a 30 second or 1-minute elevator pitch and convey its power and significance is I believe impossible. If you pushed me, the most concise thing I'd say is:

"Pioneering Leadership requires you to be extremely open-minded. It is the most powerful strategy in the world, that can be used by virtually anyone to create a better future: better lives, better careers, better businesses and organisations, better communities, countries and a better world. It is estimated that it is only used by 1% of the population. It is the opposite of business as usual. It involves going beyond the mainstream and best practice, beyond the leading edge of progress, human endeavour and enterprise, and involves challenging the status quo, being first, new, different and better, using new thinking and new ideas to create new solutions, taking new actions in new ways, that result in new, different and better outcomes and things. Its secret ingredient is imagination, which Einstein said was more important than knowledge. It offers the prospect of infinite potential, possibility and opportunity. It can be used to make the seemingly impossible possible, solve difficult problems in unique ways, create and exploit exciting opportunities, compete against tough competition and win, and achieve extraordinary things, drive progress and move the human race forward. The real secret to Pioneering Leadership is that it embraces the infinite whole, and is unconstrained by the limits that exist in knowledge and in the mainstream today."

Can You See the Possibility, Potential and Opportunity That Pioneering Leadership Offers You?

Many years ago, while studying psychology, I learnt that two people may see the same thing, yet perceive it and understand it in very different ways, it can be seen in politics, where different parties can have completely different views on what is right and what is wrong, what is good and what is bad. Understanding Pioneering Leadership is not simply a question of understanding the logic that underpins it, but being able to see the possibility, potential and opportunity it offers you. If you honestly "get it", it should create a light bulb moment, where you see clearly, what you didn't see before. Pioneering Leadership has always been there for you, available to be used, but you've possibly not been aware of it or ever had it in your top of mind awareness.

Chapter 5

The Four Preliminary Steps Prior to Practicing Pioneering Leadership

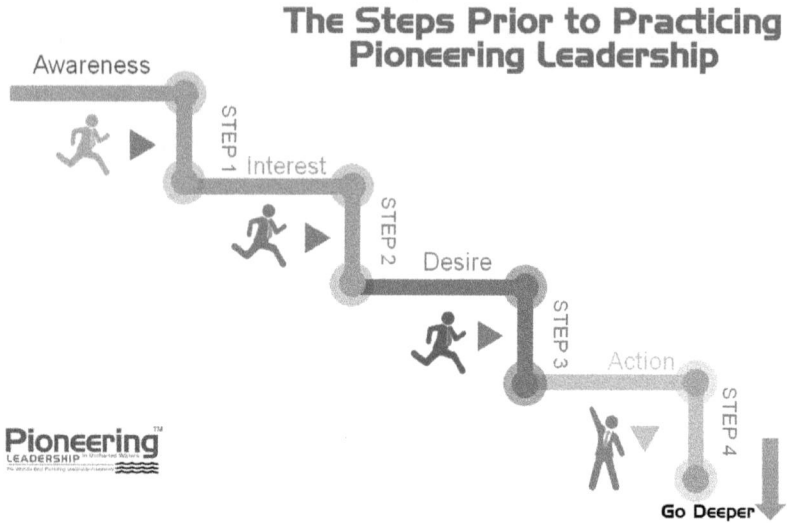

The Steps Prior to Practicing Pioneering Leadership

Awareness

STEP 1

Interest

STEP 2

Desire

STEP 3

Action

STEP 4

Pioneering
LEADERSHIP

Go Deeper

Before trying to use Pioneering Leadership, you need to go through the 4 preliminary steps, which are designed to get you to the Pioneering Leadership start line. If you are not aware of Pioneering Leadership's existence, or if it doesn't make it to your top of mind awareness, you are never going even to consider using it. Having brought it to your top of mind awareness, you've got to be interested enough to learn more about it. Having learnt more about it, you need to want to use it, and that want or desire has to be strong enough, to make you take action and use it, and stick with it through the tough times.

The Core of The Pioneering Leadership in Uncharted Waters™ Framework

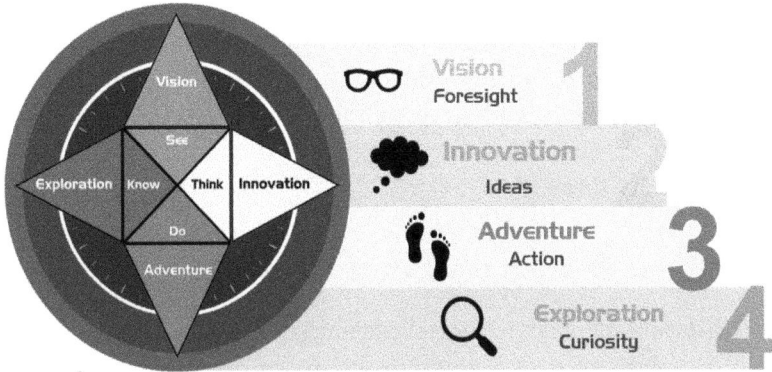

The Pioneering Leadership in Uncharted Waters Framework Core™

I

The Core of the Pioneering Leadership in Uncharted Waters Framework

At the heart and centre of the Pioneering Leadership in Uncharted Waters Framework is the core, where Pioneering Leadership happens. When you use it, you get to become a Pioneering Leader and:

1. A Visionary.

2. An Innovator.

3. An Adventurer.

4. An Explorer.

Becoming these things, you can challenge the status quo, to break the mould, change the game, blaze a trail, positively disrupt and achieve extraordinary things that may be beyond your wildest dreams. You get to use the most powerful strategy on earth, to harness infinite potential, possibility and opportunity, to make the seemingly impossible possible, to solve difficult problems in unique ways, to create and exploit exciting opportunities, to compete against tough competition and win, to create extraordinary things and to drive progress and move the human race forward.

Get Others to Do It for You If You Want

The best leaders can harness the talents, skills and strengths of others. We can't be good at everything; all our strengths have equal and opposite weaknesses.

You can be a natural Non-Pioneering Leader and learn to use Pioneering Leadership, but alternatively you can either harness Pioneering Leaders within your organisation if you identify them and if they are any, or hire some on a permanent, temporary or consultancy basis.

It is often hard for Natural Pioneering Leaders in Organisations to be taken seriously and respected as a Pioneering Leader, if they have previously been working in conventional ways as a Non-Pioneering Leader.

Without authority and support, it is easy for any Pioneering Leaders who are not in charge to be blocked and demotivated and to leave.

It is possible to hire Pioneering Leaders and the very person hiring them to clash, as Pioneering Leadership meets Non-Pioneering Leadership. Such clashes are less likely to happen if clear terms of reference and authority are established. People often hire consultants to be told what they want to hear. Pioneering Leadership questions and challenges the status quo and that can be uncomfortable for many people, whose response could be defensive at best and aggressive at worst.

Don't expect to hire a Pioneering Leader and have them tell you what you want to hear, they might, but they might not. No two Pioneering Leaders will be the same. Hire two different Pioneering Leaders to do the same job and they could take diametrically opposite approaches. Pioneering Leaders have a habit of turning things on their head, seeing things from different perspectives and thinking things that most others don't.

You can also hire a Pioneering Leader as a mentor to help you navigate and execute Pioneering Leadership.

"Pioneering Leadership is one of humanities biggest secrets. It is the most powerful strategy on earth and offers unlimited possibility, potential and opportunity - perhaps you should think about using it?"

Chapter 6

Attention

Chapter 6

Attention Grabbers - 10 Big Fat Claims to Get Your Attention

A great many years ago, while working for the Mobil Oil Corporation, which was then the world's fourth largest company, I remember being sent on a sales training course, where the sales trainer taught us when canvassing new clients, to state a big bold claim that sounds like it is not true but is.

The reason is, that in the modern age we are all typically so extraordinary busy and our time is finite, we only get 24 hours in the day, and everyone is trying to take a bit of time and attention from us. They are doing it in person, online, on the telephone, in the mail and as if that is not enough, we are bombarded with messages, from advertising billboards to packaging of goods in the supermarket, and on social media.

Newspapers know this, which is why they tempt us with catchy, sometimes controversial headlines, and strap lines to make us read more, Facebook has mastered feeding us messages and adverts that all try to influence us. Have you noticed the online ads that do the same thing? Everywhere we go, there are channels of communication blasting us with stuff, most of which we don't want and don't care about, but what if amongst that, was something precious; a winning lottery ticket buried in a pile of papers, an opportunity of a lifetime, a secret that could change everything, our lives, our careers, our businesses or organisations, our countries, our communities or even something that could save the whole world?

What the sales trainer was saying that the big bold claim is like an elevator pitch, a tiny bit of time to make an impact and get a result. The great thing about big bold claims that people don't believe is that they find it very difficult when put on the spot to not say: "prove it". When they say that, you've just got valuable permission to deliver your pitch. Most things that sound too good to be true, usually aren't real. When Pioneering Leadership works well, the most extraordinary things, beyond your wildest dreams are possible, but it doesn't always work; results and outcomes are not known, and by its very nature, it involves risks and uncertainty. For many, that is reason enough to ignore it, but in doing so, you are choosing to rule out, the single thing that has had the biggest impact on your life, because Pioneering Leadership is the driving force of progress, responsible for the very best things in the world today. It was Pioneering leadership that took us out of horses and carriages and into cars, and into jet planes. The results of pioneering leadership are everywhere including science, medicine, technology, education, communication, engineering, government, sport, entertainment, the military etc. Virtually all the greatest people who have ever lived were/are Pioneering Leaders. The greatest and most extraordinary people are not status quo people, they are people who were different and better, which made them extraordinary, as opposed to ordinary.

To remind you of just how incredibly Pioneering Leadership can be, I am going to give you 10 big fat claims about it, that might seem like they are not true to begin with, but are true. You might need to use these when pitching Pioneering Leadership to colleagues, or to convince yourself to learn more.

Discover	1. The Most Powerful Strategy on Earth.
Harness	2. Unlimited Possibility, Potential and Opportunity.
Reveal	3. A secret that can change positively everything.
Make	4. The seemingly impossible possible.
Solve	5. Difficult problems or challenges in unique ways.
Create & Exploit	6. Exciting opportunities.
Compete	7. Compete against tough competition and win.
Achieve	8. Achieve extraordinary things.
Drive and Move	9. Drive progress and move the human race forwards.
Recognise	10. Probably one of the most important things in your life.

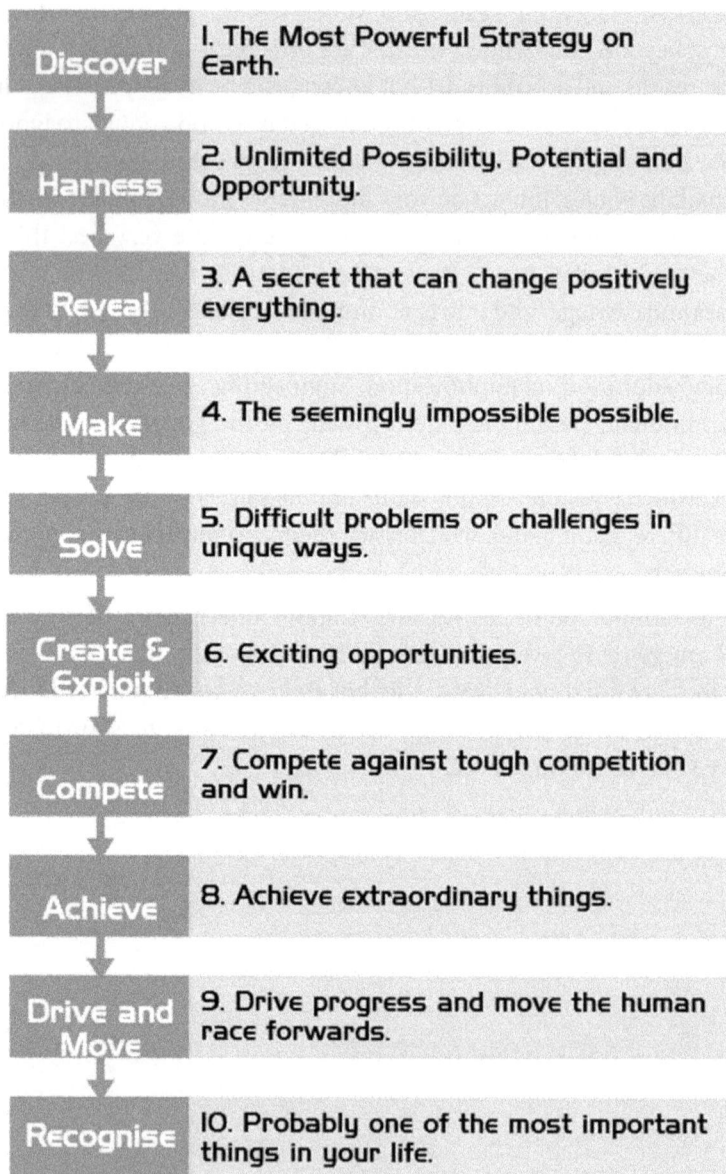

10 Big Fat Claims That Are True

Attention Grabber -Big Fat Claim One

The most powerful strategy on earth and it is available to you

" There is Nothing More Powerful than Pioneering Leadership"

What makes Pioneering Leadership different to all other strategies, is that it is a high-level strategy and modus operandi, that is pretty much applicable to all people in all circumstances, involved in all activities, endeavours and enterprise, and as such, it is as applicable for a private individual as it is for world leaders.

At this high level, there are only two strategy choices:

1.   Pioneering Leadership (used by estimated 1% of people)

2. Non-Pioneering Leadership (used by estimated 100% of people)

Pioneering Leadership is the most powerful of the two and is responsible for most of the greatest achievements in human history. Non-Pioneering Leadership is oriented primarily to knowledge whereas Pioneering Leadership embraces unlimited imagination as well as knowledge. Einstein says: "Imagination is more important than knowledge". Pioneering Leadership represent the whole, whereas non-pioneering leadership represents a part, and the whole is always more than the part!

Attention Grabber -Big Fat Claim Two

Access unlimited potential, possibility and opportunity

"Pioneering Leadership offers you unlimited, possibility, potential
and opportunity."

Chapter 6

If Pioneering Leadership truly offered you unlimited possibility, potential and opportunity, why would you choose to ignore it and settle for less? Pioneering Leadership makes available everything including, that which currently doesn't exist today or hasn't been done before.

Attention Grabber -Big Fat Claim Three

The Biggest Secret That Can Make the Biggest Difference to You, Others and the World.

"Pioneering Leadership is the biggest secret that could make the biggest difference to you, others and the world."

Chapter 6

"It's classified, I could tell you, but then I'd have to kill you".

Tom Cruise in the film Top Gun

With the internet and communications technology in all forms, from the humble book, through to a plethora of different types of media, humanity has never before had access to such vast amounts of knowledge and information. It is difficult to conceive that it is possible for big secrets to exist still. We assume that we'll be taught the most important things and like cream rising to the top of a bottle of milk that the most important things will find their way to our top of mind awareness.

At the time this book was written, Pioneering Leadership had the lowest profile imaginable, there were very few books about it, incredibly few people were teaching it, and it doesn't appear on the curriculum of most of the world's leading universities and teaching establishments. In December 2017, there were less than 200 searches for it on Google per month, worldwide.

Pioneering Leadership is incredibly low profile, it never registers on most people's personal radar, they don't know about it, recognise it for what it is, let alone use it. That is surprising, because it is arguably the single thing, that could make the biggest difference to, you, others and the wider world.

Attention Grabber -Big Fat Claim Four

Make the seemingly impossible – possible

"Pioneering Leadership can make the seemingly impossible – possible"

You might be familiar with the Mission Impossible film franchise, starring Tom Cruise, where he takes on missions that all ordinary people would think to be impossible, but against all the odds, he succeeds. This might be fiction, but Pioneering Leadership makes things like this possible in real life; things like sending men to the moon, communicating at the speed of light, creating a virtual city of over a million people airborne in aeroplanes at any one-time, transplanting hearts from people who have just died to other people whose hearts are just about to fail completely.

John Harrison was a self-educated British clockmaker living in the 1700's, who took on the seemingly impossible challenge of creating a chronograph, which was accurate enough to enable mariners to accurately establish longitude at sea. He spent most of his life dedicated to the problem, and in a BBC Public Poll in 2002, he was voted 39th on the list of 100 Greatest Britons.

History is full of people who have made the seemingly impossible – possible. You can use Pioneering Leadership as they did and join their esteemed ranks.

What do you want to do? Create immense wealth, make a massive contribution to humanity, solve difficult problems, create things that others don't believe is possible, create world peace, eliminate poverty, cure cancer? It doesn't have to be something spectacular on a global scale; it can merely be achieving things that seem impossible to you right now.

Attention Grabber -Big Fat Claim Five

You can solve difficult problems and challenges
in unique ways

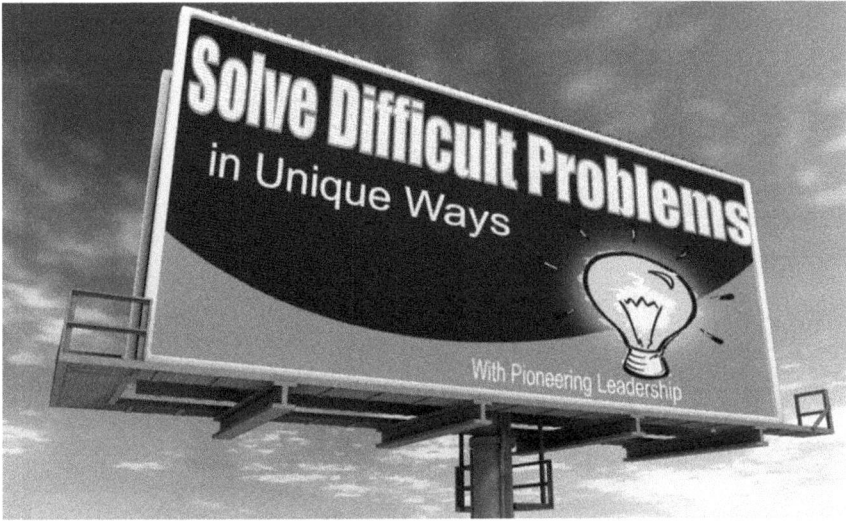

When electricity was first discovered and put to use, there were huge problems with power distribution that Nikola Tesla solved with his invention of AC (alternating current). When American athlete Dick Fosbury, invented a new high jump technique called the Fosbury Flop, it changed the sport of high jump, and everyone else started using it.

During the Second World War, there were countless examples of Pioneering Leadership being used in the theatre of war. The British Special Air Service was formed as a tiny commando force, initially of 5 officers and 60 other ranks to operate behind enemy lines in the North African Campaign. Using stealth, they blew up enemy planes on the runway, and disappeared before the enemy could catch them; they have since become a legendary force. In separate operations, this time on the water, a group of British Royal Marines, who came to be known as the Cockleshell Heroes, led an audacious raid against enemy ships, transferring from a submarine into canvas-covered canoes, paddling under cover of darkness to plant explosives on ships. Their endeavours led to the formation of the British Special Boat Service.

The human ingenuity of the few has provided unique solutions to difficult problems and challenges throughout human history. You can use Pioneering Leadership to help you to solve difficult problems in unique ways if you want to. "Insanity is doing the same things and expecting a different result".

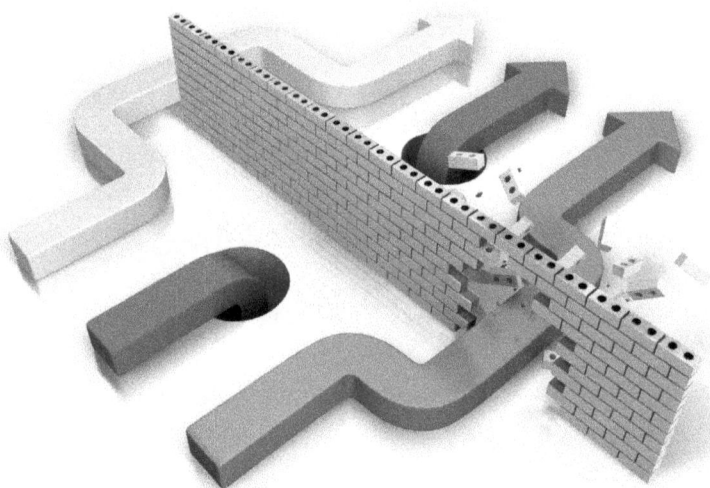

Attention Grabber -Big Fat Claim Six

Create and Exploit exciting opportunities

"Pioneering Leadership enables you to create and exploit exciting opportunities."

In every field of human endeavour, there are those who use Pioneering Leadership to create and exploit exciting opportunities, that result in better lives, better careers, better businesses and organisations, better communities, better countries and a better world.

You too can use Pioneering Leadership, to help you to create and exploit exciting opportunities. Pioneering leadership provides the possibility of maximum opportunity, so if you don't want to settle for second best, you know what you need to use.

Albert Einstein, Steve Jobs, Bill Gates, Mark Zuckerberg, Elon Musk, Sir Richard Branson, Jeff Bezos and countless more have all had the courage to use it to create maximum opportunity.

Attention Grabber - Big Fat Claim Seven

Compete against tough competition and win

"Use Pioneering Leadership to compete against tough competition and win."

We love the story of the underdog who triumphed, the person who apparently stood no chance at all, who came out the victor. The Wright Brothers, who were first to successfully achieve powered flight, were prime examples. They had many competitors, who wanted to be first to achieve the first powered flight. The most high profile, and the only one with government funding was the secretary of the Smithsonian, Samuel Pierpont Langley.

Pioneering Leadership has little respect for money or status, it is all about challenging the status quo and as a result of that, frequently results in being able to compete against the toughest competition and win.

You can be the David who beats the giant Goliath, in whatever field of endeavour you are in. With Pioneering Leadership on your side, the fiercest competitors should be quaking in their boots!

Compete Against Tough **Competition and Win!**

PIONEERING **LEADERSHIP**

Attention Grabber - Big Fat Claim Eight

Achieve extraordinary things

"Non-Pioneering Leaders represent 99% of the population and Pioneering Leaders just 1%. Being different to everyone else, provides the opportunity to achieve extraordinary things rather than ordinary things."

Chapter 6

Attention Grabber - Big Fat Claim Nine

Drive progress and move humanity forward

Albert Einstein

Nelson Mandela

Winston Churchill

Mahatma Gandhi

Pioneering Leaders have the potential to achieve extraordinary things and drive progress and move humanity forwards in ways that Non-Pioneering Leaders don't. They can be positive or negative and frequently polarise opinions.

Attention Grabber - Big Fat Claim Ten

The biggest thing in your life

"Pioneering Leadership is like an elephant in the room. It is the biggest thing in your life but you probably don't see it."

Pioneering Leadership's impact is everywhere. If you were to be able to go back four or five generations in your family, you'd discover that their lives and the world, was very different to how it is today. Somewhat unusually, my dad was conceived when his dad was seventy years old. He was born in 1865, before the motor car, before electricity, aeroplanes, wireless communication etc. and he lived when author Charles Dickens was still alive. There has been a lot of change since then; what is normal today is the result of Pioneering Leadership. What is certain, is that change and progress will never stop, and the most significant changes are likely to be the result of Pioneering Leadership. It is highly likely to impact you and your family in possibly profound ways. It may save your life, improve your life or make the world a better place. It is likely to show up in every part of your life, whether you recognise it or not. It could be an even bigger thing if you chose to use it yourself, rather than be impacted by the Pioneering Leadership of others.

"In any endeavour anywhere involving anyone there are just two high level strategy choices:

1. Pioneering Leadership or

2. Non-Pioneering Leadership"

Chapter 7

Interest

Interesting Facts and Information

Chapter 7

I f you are natural Pioneering Leader, you are likely to recognise Pioneering Leadership for what it is; the framework is likely to appear logical and straightforward to you and should help you to be a better Pioneering Leader. If you are not a Natural Pioneering Leader, the framework will reveal the secrets of Pioneering Leadership and an actionable approach so that you too can use Pioneering Leadership.

Pioneering Leaders are sometimes seen positively and sometimes negatively by Non-Pioneering Leaders. Pioneering Leaders can deliver extraordinary things, but success can never be guaranteed, and there is always a flip side; there are usually pros and cons to everything and Pioneering Leadership is no exception. When Pioneering Leadership succeeds, it can be perceived as the best thing since sliced bread, but when it fails, it can seem like the worse thing ever.

I seek to show you the truth as I have discovered it to be. The framework is intended to place Pioneering Leadership in the context of traditional approaches to things. You'll learn that there is an inter-dependence between the two, both are needed, and both are valuable in their own way.

Don't expect this book to only focus on the positive aspects of Pioneering Leadership. There are no rose-coloured glasses or purely positive spin, but the framework provides for realism and objectivity.

There is likely to be something about you or your situation, that is making you read this now, which is also going to make you venture into uncharted waters. It could be that you, your business, organisation, community, country or others have huge pain or a big problem or challenge to solve, or that you are interested in creating and exploiting exciting opportunities, driving change, transformation or improvement. Perhaps your heart and soul is pulling you towards living an extraordinary life where you get to make a massive contribution to others or that you have an instinct that there must be better ways and better things.

The truth is that following others is the ordinary life path, not the extraordinary one. Some people perceive the ordinary path to be the safe one, but many historical events have shown us that we humans are always at risk of blindly following each other over metaphorical cliffs like lemmings or sheep. You've got to be clear on what you want and why. There is nothing wrong with following the ordinary path, you just need to decide whether it is the path you want to take. You can't be extraordinary and achieve extraordinary things by being ordinary and doing ordinary things in an ordinary way.

While you think about that, I'd like to suggest that you ponder on the following:

There is not a single thing in the universe that holds more possibilities, more potential and more opportunities."

The chances are, that unless you are the rare one in every hundred or so people, you are unlikely:

1. To know what it is.

2. To be interested in it.

3. To recognise it for what it is. and

4. To use it, and if and when you do use it, you probably won't realise you are using it.

The Pioneering Leadership in Uncharted Waters Framework seeks to provide answers, knowledge and know-how, to help you make decisions regarding Pioneering Leadership.

At the time of writing this book, you are unlikely to find it taught at most schools, universities or business schools or indeed virtually anywhere, yet it is likely to be the one thing that has the greatest impact on your life; because it is the one thing that is mostly responsible for progress and the status quo in every field of human endeavour today. At the time this book was written, there were less than 100 searches a month on Google for it. I hope to change that statistic.

Chapter 7

It is more valuable than all the knowledge in the world combined. The incredible thing is that it is available to you and you can use it do and achieve a myriad of different things including:

1. To solve problems and overcome challenges.

2. To create and exploit opportunities.

3. To drive progress.

4. To positively move humanity forward.

What is particularly surprising is that you can use it across virtually every type of human endeavour/activity possible, for yourself, for others, for organisations, and to create better lives, better careers, better businesses and organisations, better communities, better countries and a better world.

Imagine if it were possible to create a list of all the scales that exist in the world and also a list of all those that could exist, with a scale meaning something that is used to measure or compare the level of something. Include all the ones that matter most to you, which perhaps might include scales of:

1. Failure to Success.

2. Bad to Good.

3. Low Achievement to the Highest Achievement.

4. Losing to Winning.

5. Poverty to Wealth.

6. Illness to Heath.

7. War and Peace.

8. Sadness to Happiness etc.

9. Ordinary to Extraordinary.

10. Despair to Pure Joy.

11. Unsustainability to sustainability.

12. Similarity to Disruption.

It is the one thing that is most likely to enable you to achieve the very best result on whatever scale you choose; think of extremely good things!

> *"You might recognise it under many different names and different guises; its effect is everywhere, and it shapes the entire world and your life in the most profound ways, but the chances are you've never truly recognised it, or seen it for what it is. You might have even used it without recognising its name. Pioneering Leadership is "the thing"; the most Powerful Strategy available to Humanity and a lot more besides".*

I dare you to challenge these claims because you'll discover that they are true. You'll discover that the whole of anything can never be less than a part of it. Read on to discover what that simple fact means for you.

Non-Pioneering Leadership Versus Pioneering Leadership

Pioneering Leadership
The Opposite Of Business as Usual

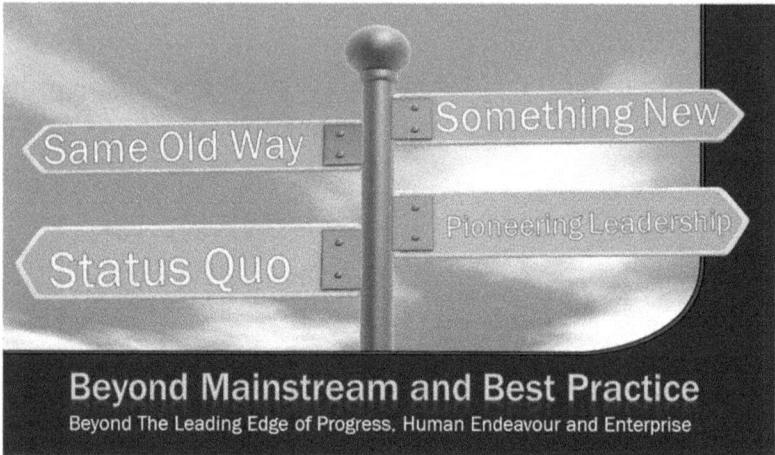

Same Old Way

Something New

Status Quo

Pioneering Leadership

Beyond Mainstream and Best Practice
Beyond The Leading Edge of Progress, Human Endeavour and Enterprise

Pioneering Leadership and Non-Pioneering Leadership are Polar Opposites

Without having clarity about the difference between Non-Pioneering Leadership, which is used by approximately 99% of People, 99% of the time and Pioneering Leadership which is used by just 1% of people, you are likely to remain stuck in a world where Non-Pioneering Leadership is your default and only option. The only exception is if you are a Natural (Born), Pioneering Leader; if you are one of those you are likely to be infinitely more successful if you have clarity about the differences and also understand why you sometimes might clash with Non-Pioneering Leaders.

Non-Pioneering Leadership	Pioneering Leadership
1. Business as Usual.	1. Opposite of Business as Usual.
2. What 99% do.	2. What 1% or less do.
3. Maintains Status Quo.	3. Challenges Status Quo.
4. Lesser Possibilities, Potential and Opportunities.	4. Greatest Possibilities, Potential and Opportunities.
5. Path: Known, Proven, Tried and Tested.	5. Path: Unknown, Unproven, Untried and Untested into Uncharted Waters.
6. Part of Mainstream and Strives towards Best Practice.	6. Strives Beyond Mainstream and Best Practice.
7. Ordinary Approach	7. Extraordinary Approach
8. Based Predominantly on Knowledge	8. Based on Knowledge + Unlimited Imagination
9. Largely Conforms to Norms, Follows, Rules, Conventions, Seniors and Others.	9. Likes to Not Conform to Norms, Test, Challenge and Sometimes Breaks Rules, Conventions and Authority.
10. Short Terms Results More Predictable.	10. Short-Term Results – Less Predictable.
11. Perceived as Lower Risk.	11. Perceived as Higher Risk.

12. Not Perceived as Threatening to Individuals and Organisations.	12. More Likely to be Perceived as Threatening to Individuals, Organisations, and Authority and Power Structures.
13. Less Likely to Fail	13. More Likely to Fail
14. Highs Likely to Be Lower and Lows Less Low.	14. Highs Likely to be Higher and Lows Lower.
15. Mostly in Line with People's Expectations.	15. Mostly Different to What People Expect.
16. Mostly Closed Agenda.	16. Mostly Open Agenda.
17. Few Surprises.	17. Many Surprises.
18. Typically, Slower Rate of Change and Extent of Change.	18. Typically, Faster Rate of Change, with Possibility for Transformation, Disruption, Game Changing, Breaking the Mould, Changing the Game, Blazing New Trails.
19. Typically, More Stable and Reliable.	19. Typically, More Unstable and Less Reliable.
20. Less Likely to Be Able to Make Seemingly Impossible Possible.	20. Can Make Seemingly Impossible Possible.
21. Less Likely to Solve Difficult Problems in Unique Ways.	21. Can Solve Difficult Problems in Unique Ways.

22. Less Likely to Create and Exploit Exciting Opportunities	22. Can Create and Exploit Exciting Opportunities.
23. Less Likely to Create Progress and Move Human Race Forwards	23. More Likely to Create Progress and Move Human Race Forwards.
24. Less Likely to be Able to Compete Against Tough Competition and Win.	24. More Likely to be Able to Compete Against Tough Competition and Win.
25. Path of the Ordinary	25. Path of the Extraordinary.
26. Followers of the Most Significant Changes	26. Initiators of The Most Significant Change.
27. Low Threshold for Failure.	27. High Threshold for Failure Which is Inevitable on Path to Greatest Success.
28. More Likely to Seek and Achieve Short-Term Return on Investment	28. Less Likely to Seek or Be Able to Deliver Short-Term Return on Investment
29. Often Thwarted by Obstacles, Challenges and Threats.	29. Motivated and Energised by Obstacles, Challenges and Threats.
30. Fits into Recognised Moulds.	30. Less Likely to Fit into Moulds other than Pioneering Leadership Moulds.

Dame Stephanie Shirley Example

Highly successful technology entrepreneur and philanthropist, Dame Stephanie Shirley, who escaped the horror of the Nazi Holocaust as an unaccompanied child refugee on Kindertransport, kindly gave me a copy of her autobiography called "Let it Go". She described taking on a Non-Pioneering Leader Managing Director, saying: "she had little interest in – or flair for creativity or innovation, but she thrived on the less strategic aspects of the business, on making the right things happen day-to-day. She was organised, strong-minded, calm, principled, a good communicator and good at dealing with pressure". She contrasted this with herself, a Pioneering Leader. "My talent is for being an entrepreneur, in the widest sense. I love thinking of new ideas, questioning first principles, sensing new opportunities, starting things, changing things, recruiting new teams, attacking new challenges. That kind of work, for me, is indistinguishable from pleasure."

I feel the same about the things she mentions as she does. My Wealth Dynamics Profile report says: "You need to maximise your time invested in dreaming up and creating new ideas, products and strategies. Yes, that is right, doing things that are the most fun."

Pioneering Leaders need Non-Pioneering Leaders and vice versa. Pioneering Leaders know this more than Non-Pioneering Leaders, who frequently don't even know that Pioneering Leaders exist, and who often feel they are doing just fine without them.

Don't Mistake Maintaining The Status Quo As No Change

People often mistake the phrase "maintaining the status Quo" as meaning no change, but that is not the case. We live in a world of continual change, so most people are having to change, whether they want to or not.

Many organisations see themselves as being very innovative, implementing perhaps the latest technology and adopting the latest efficient working practices and processes. This isn't pioneering if lots of other people in similar situation are doing the same thing.

Most Non-Pioneering Leaders aren't stuck in the Dark Ages; they are probably growing, developing, learning, innovating and being successful, perhaps highly successful. Non-Pioneering Leaders often benchmark against others and strive towards "Best Practice" in all that they do. It would be foolish to argue that this is not a good strategy, it clearly is. However, Pioneering Leaders seek to be better than Best Practice today; they strive towards doing what has not been done before or doing things in new ways. They set new standards, they lead the way that others often follow, and whatever anyone else achieves, they look to achieve more and better. They may or may not succeed in their quest. It should be remembered that Non-Pioneering Leaders also may or may not succeed.

On Rogers Diffusion of Innovation Curve, he had "pioneers" as the first 2 ½% to adopt and use an innovation. Pioneers in "Pioneering Leadership" terms, are the ones who create the innovation in the first place. Different people can interpret Pioneering Leadership in different ways. Innovation is often used interchangeably with Pioneering, but they are different; not all innovation is Pioneering, but successful Pioneering is always innovative. If you are discussing Pioneering Leadership with other people, it might be prudent to refer to Pioneering Leadership in Uncharted Waters Framework to avoid misunderstanding.

In most cases continual change is normal; it is what everyone does. Pioneering Leaders are the ones who do what others don't. Why does each of us do anything? There are always reasons, and the biggest reasons are, that we do what we are told, what we are taught, what we see others are doing etc. We are all unique individuals, but we are also social beings that need to fit in and belong. What happened to weird children at school who didn't fit in, they probably got bullied or teased.

We remember that. Pioneering Leaders are frequently seen as either cool like Steve Jobs or Weird because they are different. It takes serious courage to be deliberately different and not fit in with the expectations of others.

Dismal Failure and Ultimate Success

Pioneering Leadership Can Result in Dismal Failure or Supreme Success

On February 7th, 2005, a 28-year-old British Yachtswomen, Ellen Macarthur, became the fastest person to sail around the world, beating the previous record by over a day. The BBC extended the Ten O'clock News to cover the story with a massive 5.7million peak viewing.

When she made her triumphant return to Falmouth in the UK, thousands of people and media from all over the world were there to greet her. Due to her achievement, she was made the UK's youngest Dame.

The BBC paid for me to travel to Falmouth and put me up in a hotel overnight as I was to be a guest on their news coverage, eventually being interviewed on the deck/trampolines of her record-breaking trimaran vessel because I had helped her early in her career.

During my BBC TV interview, I talked about Ellen's achievement and the public's reaction to her success. I spoke of the "Power of the Spirit of Adventure" that Ellen and her entire team had demonstrated. I described an Adventure as "A venture involving risk and uncertainty in the hope of positive outcomes with the expectation of excitement". Pioneering Leadership is an Adventure.

Ellen and her team used Pioneering Leadership to achieve extraordinary success, but it was in stark contrast to her earlier efforts to raise sponsorship, where thousands of letters received no attention, and when her first ocean race resulted in a commendable 17th place.

Fellow British yachtsman, Pete Goss, secured £4m in sponsorship and designed and built a pioneering new catamaran called Team Philips, which he intended to use to win a round the world yacht race. Sadly, during trials, the yacht started to break up in the North Atlantic and had to be abandoned.

Pioneering Leadership offers the prospect of both dismal failure and ultimate success. There can be no sugar coating it; success isn't guaranteed using it, failure remains a distinct possibility. Not only does failure represent a real threat, but many challenges often have to be overcome on the path to eventual success.

There is a saying: "nothing ventured – nothing gained". If you don't accept the risk and uncertainty that Pioneering Leadership offers, you can't expect the ultimate success, which Pioneering Leaders like Ellen Macarthur, Einstein, Steve Jobs, Mark Zuckerberg and all the others have achieved.

Chapter 7

Everyone would like to have the prizes, riches, fame, respect, recognition of Pioneering Leadership success, but few would want to feel the pain, misery, humiliation and suffering of failure, with dreams and hopes going up in smoke.

It is often failure that spurns Pioneering Leaders on; they are the ones who, if they fall off the metaphoric horse, with get straight back on, wiser and more determined than ever. Entrepreneurs who are Pioneering Leaders, often go bust and lose everything, and then find a way of finding success. Billionaire entrepreneur Richard Branson has many failed businesses under his belt. Often failure is a better teacher than success.

> *"Anyone who has never made a mistake has never tried anything new."*
>
> *Albert Einstein*

> *"Success is not final, failure is not fatal: it is the courage to continue that counts."*
>
> *"Success is the ability to go from failure to failure without losing your enthusiasm."*
>
> *Winston S. Churchill*

I was once interview by Richard Branson's Virgin for an article about a trend in the business world, where failures are admitted to and even celebrated.

With Pioneering Leadership failure and success go hand in hand, you've got to be prepared for both.

Many businesses are driven by short-term profit results and leaders remunerated accordingly, which means there is little appetite to take risks in the hope of more significant gain. Anticipated return on capital employed as a means of investment appraisal, is likely to exclude anything that involves Pioneering Leadership continually. In the short term, this strategy may be sound, but it is likely to accelerate long-term business failure. Many big organisations see Pioneering Leadership like an equivalent of Casino Gambling, yet at the same time, look in envy at the stratospheric success of Pioneering organisations, like many of the biggest tech companies.

Business Angels will often back the Pioneering Leaders, knowing that one good successful investment can often compensate for ten or more that fail. Often Pioneering Leaders can't get support for their Pioneering within large organisations; they are usually the ones who create competing start-up ventures, which have which have the potential to disrupt markets and provide the biggest organisations with the most significant threats.

"The Staff at Virgin have a name for me. It is "Dr Yes".
They call me this because I won't say no. I find more
reasons to do things than not do them. My motto really is
"Screw it – Let's do it"

Billionaire Entrepreneur Richard Branson

When resources are tight and pressure for results is high, it can be tempting to not take risks. Voluntarily taking risks, instinctively seems bad to many Boards, it seems much better to approve investment proposals with a solid Return on Capital Employed (ROCE) and low risk and chance of failure. When you start excluding pretty much everything where the outcome is uncertain, you correspondingly turn off the most significant potential opportunities and take Pioneering Leadership off the table permanently. Ironically not taking risks is the biggest risk that any business or organisation could probably make.

Conflict and Harmony Between Pioneering Leaders and Non-Pioneering Leaders

There can be conflict or harmony between Pioneering and Non-Pioneering Leaders

There can be both harmony and conflict between Pioneering Leaders and Non-Pioneering Leaders depending on the circumstances involved. While Pioneering Leaders can drive progress and move humanity forward, and while what is normal today, was often the result of Pioneering Leadership in the past, there remains the reality that Pioneering Leadership and Non-Pioneering Leadership are frequently complete opposites. Sometimes opposites will attract and sometimes they will clash and repel.

Harvard Professor, Clayton Christensen coined the phrase "Innovators Dilemma".

"Clayton Christensen demonstrates how successful, outstanding companies can do everything "right" and yet still lose their market leadership – or even fail – as new, unexpected competitors rise and take over the market".
Wikipedia

Companies who use Pioneering Leadership can threaten their core business with new pioneering innovations.

Pioneering Leaders provide the biggest threat to the Non-Pioneering Leader establishment, hierarchies and power bases, and as such, they are frequently not welcomed. They often share very different mindsets, value systems, preferences, beliefs, needs and desires to Non-Pioneering Leaders and the result can be conflict, resentment and even open hostility and civil war equivalences within organisations.

Mostly Non-Pioneering organisations often find it very difficult to attract and retain Pioneering Leaders, or to allow Pioneering Leadership to flourish and be practised in their organisations.

It can be very irritating, if you are a Non-Pioneering Leader who was a diligent student at school, who worked hard, got good grades, went to a top university, studied hard learning from top professors, who are masters of knowledge, and work hard in your career, doing all the right things, follow all the rules to meet a Pioneering Leader who did none of what you did and earns a hundred times more than you.

Gary Dutton is a Pioneering Leader and entrepreneur, who I helped to write and publish his autobiography. He left school at 16 with no qualifications; his teacher said he would never amount to anything. Last time I checked he was worth about £130m, he had a fleet of luxury cars including a shiny red Ferrari soft top, a Rolls Royce, an Executive Jet and his only little mini cruise ship that he is qualified to skipper. Pioneering Leader and Billionaire, Richard Branson had dyslexia and at times has struggled to know the difference between gross and net or one end of the balance sheet from the other. Billionaire Pioneering

Leader college dropouts include Michael Dell (Dell Computers), Steve Jobs (Apple), Bill Gates (Microsoft), Mark Zuckerberg (Facebook) and Larry Ellison (Oracle).

Pioneering Leaders don't see things, think, know or act like Non-Pioneering Leaders. It is hardly surprising if there are sometimes conflicts between the two.

Pioneering Leaders, being the minority, frequently feel the most frustrated, misunderstood, and not valued, but Pioneering Leaders can be difficult, obstinate, single-minded, sometimes self-centered and not prepared to listen to the views of others, particularly Non-Pioneering Leaders. Pioneering Leader, Steve Jobs even got fired from Apple the company that he had co-founded, before returning to save the company and put it on a path to becoming the most valuable company in the world.

Billionaire Pioneering Leader, Elon Musk was at the time this book was written under immense pressure with his company Tesla struggling with production and cash flow issues. Non-Pioneering Leader outsiders are applying their Non-Pioneering values in their judgement of him and the effect is almost explosive. Pioneering Leaders are different, and sparks can fly, when the differences are exposed.

The difficulty is that because 99% of people are Non-Pioneering Leaders everyone understands them and ordinary Non-Pioneering Leadership, whereas Pioneering Leaders, practising Pioneering Leadership, represent a minority of just 1%, and are frequently not understood at all.

If you can learn Pioneering Leadership and recognise the differences, it makes it easier to identify potential conflicts before they arise, create boundaries and limits of authority within which Pioneering Leadership can be practised.

Knowing when to pull the plug and admit failure and defeat is always tricky, particularly when salvation and potential success seems like it could be just around the corner. Often ultimate success comes well after Non-Pioneering Leaders think you should give up. There is no easy solution to this dilemma, whatever decision is taken, you need to hope that it is the right one. It seems crazy to throw good money or resources at failed things, but equally throwing away all your investment, when you might be close to success, might seem like the dumb thing to do. It took ten years for 3M to turn the invention that led to Post It notes into a commercial success.

Cause and Effect – Possibility, Potential and Opportunity Engineering to get the best results

One of the most important things you need to open your mind to, is that there are high-level principles of cause and effect that are generic and apply to just about everything, which means that they are relevant to you, no matter what your circumstances, your problems, your challenges, or what you want and need to accomplish. Think of Pioneering Leadership as "Possibility, Potential and Opportunity Engineering", taking the concept of "Cause and Effect Management" to the highest level to achieve the best results.

The Building Blocks of Pioneering Leadership in Uncharted Waters

There are three important building block or concepts in Pioneering Leadership in Uncharted waters that you need to understand.

Fundamentally Pioneering Leadership is about getting not just better results, but the very best results in whatever you are doing or trying to achieve and bringing into existence something which doesn't already exist.

To help bring structure to an intangible concept, I'd like to introduce three building blocks:

1. Endeavours.

2. Enterprises.

3. The Concept of Pioneering Leadership as a Modus Operandi used in endeavours and enterprises.

Endeavours

"An Endeavour is an effort to do or attain something."

You are one in 7.6 billion people (and rising) that are currently alive in the world today. You, me and everyone else belongs to what we call the human race. In every minute of every day, in every corner of the world, people are going about living their lives. At any given time, there will be people working or asleep, engaged in a leisure activity or countless other activities. Some people will be brushing their teeth, others will be cooking or doing the washing up, some will be commuting to work, others will be playing games or a sport, reading, watching TV, engaged in social media activities etc. I am sure you get the gist.

Each of the activities that we might be doing or attempting to do like work, leisure or other can be called an "Endeavour". Out of all the possible endeavours, the likelihood is that there will be other people engaged in the same or similar endeavours to ourselves. Humanity can be divided into many subsets or groups, and if we dissected the different aspects of our lives, we would see that we fit into numerous groups with other people engaged in the same endeavours, facing the same problems or challenges, often with the same or similar hopes, dreams or aspirations. We will belong to groups based on our gender, age, career vocation, nationality, skills, competencies, interests, strengths/weaknesses, personality.

Examples of Different Endeavours

If endeavours are the things we are attempting to do, there are many other ways of distinguishing ourselves.

If you take any single group based on any endeavour you will be able to organise the group in many different ways. Some examples are:

In order of:

1. Success

2. Wealth

3. Productivity

4. Efficiency

5. Effectiveness

6. Growth

7. Value Delivered / Created

8. Rewards Received

9. Difference they make

10. Recognition Received

Pioneering Leadership can help you to achieve the best at whatever you want to achieve.

Worst Outcome   **Best Outcome**

Endeavour as a Box

OPTIONS EXISTING TODAY:

Option 1   **X**

Option 2   **X**

Option 3   **X**

Option 4   **X**

Option 5 etc.   **X**

Bad Outcome   **Good Outcome**

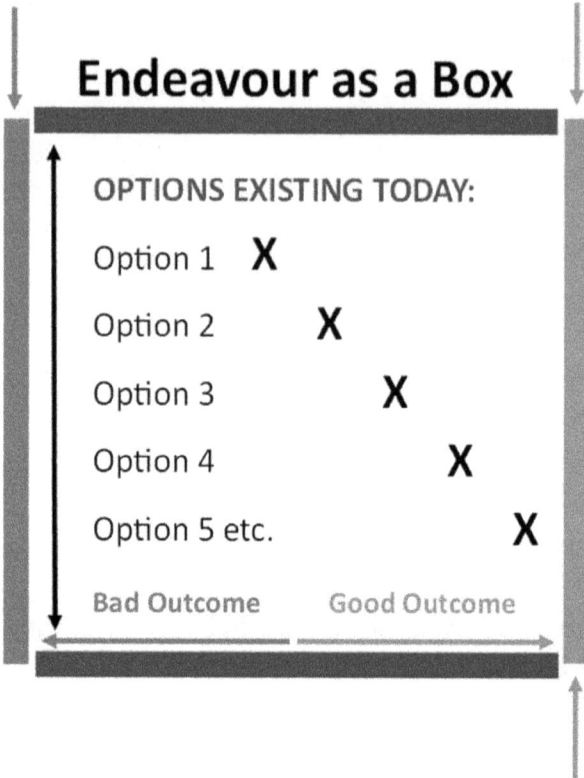

Leading Edge Today

If you take any factors or criteria of an endeavour, you can organise them into a scale of good to bad. Whatever you choose, there will be limits, e.g. limits to how good or how bad. There will be differences in the way people achieve the outcomes too. Imagine marking the boundaries and the differences as left and right borders of a box, with the top and bottom lines of the box encompassing the options/alternative approaches to achieving the desired outcome that is currently being used.

Pioneering Leaders are the ones who are obsessed with breaking out the box, to achieve better results than the best results of today, by seeing, thinking and acting differently to the majority using options that others don't.

Enterprises

"Enterprises and endeavours are similar, there are some grey areas, but for this book, an enterprise is broadly considered to be something bigger than an endeavour, e.g. an organisation, business or company or particularly difficult and important plan, project, programme or cause and may contain multiple endeavours."

Chapter 7

A business is an enterprise that exists for specific purposes like maximising shareholder value. To achieve its goal it might for example have multiple departments like sales, manufacturing, production, finance and accounting, human resources etc. Each of these departments seek to do or attain something, which we call an endeavour. Each department, in turn, has many different endeavours. The Accounting department might have various functions like Accounts Payable, Accounts Receivable, Treasury, Consolidation Accounting etc. The concept of endeavours can be taken to the lowest level of tasks carried out by individuals.

Pioneering Leadership as a High-Level Modus Operandi for Endeavours and Enterprises

"Modus Operandi is a Latin phrase that, roughly translated means: "method or mode of operating". It refers to someone's habits of working, particularly in the context of business.

An example of two different ways to achieve the result you want.

The Police sometimes refer to the abbreviation "M.O." when discussing crime and addressing the methods used by criminals.

In almost every aspect of our work and lives, we all use a particular "Modus Operandi". We mostly do this subconsciously. A well-known metaphor for the modus operandi of getting people to do things is to incentivise them with positive means to do what you want or to use the threat of punishment, a penalty of retribution if they don't do what you want. This can be referred to as a carrot or stick approach, which originated from the use of horses. Do you give them a carrot that they like as a reward for doing what you want, or do you hit them with a stick, which they don't like, to make them do it? These are two different modus operandi.

Pioneering Leadership is a Modus Operandi that can be applied to almost every endeavour, activity, situation, problem, challenge etc. Typically, when we think about doing something, we think the modus operandi relates to the specifics of what we are doing, e.g. if we are scientist doing science, we think about the details of the science involved, if we are engineers we think of the details of engineering, if we are a business person doing business, we think about the details of the business that we are doing. In this respect, there is no connection between people doing different things.

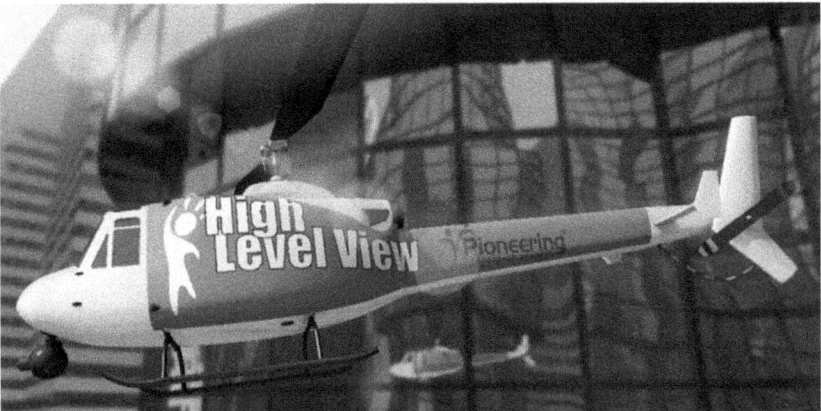

If, however, you imagine taking a helicopter or big-picture view of all these different things, you would see that there are principles, concepts, methods etc. that are common across all activities and endeavours. Whatever the activity or endeavour, the likelihood is that others will be involved in the same or similar ones. Out of all the people involved some will be higher achieving, more successful, more efficient or more anything you care to judge.

There are two crucial modus operandi, Pioneering Leadership Modus Operandi and Non-Pioneering Leadership Modus Operandi. Non-Pioneering Leaders remain in the box, while Pioneering Leaders operate out of the box as well as in the box.

Pioneering Leaders look towards the best leaders and the best practice, towards the leading edge of their particular activity or endeavour with a view of trying to figure out how they can be better or achieve better or more than the best today. They are the change makers, the people who are repelled positively from the status quo of today. Continual change is one of the few certainties in the world; the pioneers are the ones who lead that change, who strive to achieve better than the best that exists today. Pioneers don't just look to improve what already exists; they seek to create what doesn't exist at all.

Leadership itself is probably the most famous of all "Modus Operandi". Leadership is widely acknowledge as perhaps the greatest success factor of all, that can make all the difference, yet it is difficult to differentiate it from the specific activities at hand. There is a wide acceptance that Leadership is important, which is why there are a plethora of books, training courses, seminars, workshops, and speakers talking about it. You can take a great leader in something and put them in a completely different role or sector, and they are likely to be able to utilise their leadership skills and expertise in that new sector too. The principles of great leadership transcend all endeavours and enterprises as does "Pioneering Leadership", which is the ultimate game-changer.

Changing Your Defaults

In my book The Business Voyage, first published in 2005, I referred to elements of business enterprises that combine to form an overall system of operation. One of the aspects that I identified were defaults. These high level default positions frequently define a modus operandi. In any situation, we often resort to our defaults, which become hard-wired in us. They can be changed but they are difficult to change. These defaults account for why we do the things we do, but they are not limited to what we do, they include:

1. Default Beliefs

2. Default Values

3. Default Attitude

4. Default Way of Seeing Things

5. Default Way of Thinking

6. Default Way of Acting

Our defaults can be good or bad. They are usually based on our conditioning, knowledge, experience, training, what others typically do etc. It can be tempting to stick with your defaults when you achieve good results using them, but if you want to raise your aspirations and achieve even more and better things you need to consider changing your defaults. While there are as many different permutations of these things as there are people alive, it is possible to categorise them into two categories: Pioneering Leadership Category and Non-Pioneering Leadership Category.

Chapter 7

Pioneering Leadership Rules the World and Drives Progress

Continual change and progress are just about the only things you can rely on, yet both create winners and losers. As humanity moved from the industrial revolution into the high-tech revolution we are experiencing today, the rate of change and progress increased exponentially, to the extent that it is difficult to know what tomorrow will bring, let alone what things will be like in the medium and long term.

Pioneering Leadership is the primary driver of the change and progress, and it presents both enormous opportunities, but also huge threats. It is more relevant today than it has ever been in the past, and its importance is likely to increase even further, so the warning is "ignore it at your peril". You can either leverage it to your advantage, by using it, and getting it working for you, or you can default to responding to the effects of other people using it. Whether you use it yourself or others use it, the one certainty, is that it is likely to continue to impact you on an ever-increasing basis.

Pioneering Leadership is perfect, when there is uncertainty, like there is today. Rather than fear change, you can thrive on change, transformation and progress, by using Pioneering Leadership to shape a better future, and respond in the most positive way to the circumstances and factors that are beyond your control.

Chapter **8**

Desire

Build Desire – Head and Heart

You Can Build Desire with Logic and Emotion

Chapter 8

You might have a passing interest in learning about Pioneering Leadership, but there is a distinct shift needed to move from being interested in it to wanting it. If you don't want it, you'll never even try to use it. There are degrees of desire, it is not a binary thing, we might want a Ferrari, but if we want it badly enough, we might find a way of affording one. Just look at sports people who have a burning desire to win, even when faced with apparently insurmountable odds and failure, they will keep working harder, picking themselves up when they make mistakes and fail until they eventually achieve their goals. At the time this book was written, Welshman Geraint Thomas, won the world's most famous and challenging cycle race, the 2018 Tour De France. He first entered in 2007, and then finished 140th of 141 finishers. Desire is essential to make you want to use Pioneering Leadership at all, but it is also essential to make you stay with it in the tough times, especially when you face failure and setbacks.

To want anything there must be reasons, and those reasons come in two forms:

1. The Head, which is rational and logical reasons.

2. The Heart, which is emotional reasons.

In professional capacities, we sometimes like to think of ourselves as paragons of virtue, making, rational, logical decisions based on the best information and analysis, particularly when it comes to the most significant and important decisions. Experts have suggested, that the reality is that we most often make emotional decisions, based on gut feel, often with the least amount of information and without rational and objective pros and cons analysis. Having done that, we will often subconsciously reverse engineer logical justifications to support our emotional decisions.

Without realising it, we are all potentially guilty of a plethora of different biases. These biases can have profoundly positive or negative impacts on our lives. I've got a list of 100 different types of decision-making, belief, and behavioural biases. These biases can not only impact your desire to use Pioneering Leadership, but they can also affect your ability to use Pioneering Leadership effectively.

There is also a massive issue of the potential conflict between Pioneering Leadership, (used by 1%) and Non-Pioneering Leadership, (used by 99%). Pioneering Leaders, challenge, question and threaten pretty much everything that Non-Pioneering-Leaders value and find precious, believe in, stand for and do. Human nature is such that we feel completely attached to our beliefs, our values, our sense of knowing what is right and what isn't, these things can go to the core of our very identity. People will often choose to die rather than open themselves up to new beliefs and new possibilities.

If you want to consider using Pioneering Leadership when you are a natural Non-Pioneering Leader, it can honestly be challenging, but not impossible.

A Pioneering Leader merely is someone who uses Pioneering Leadership, and they are only a Pioneering Leader when they use it, not when they don't. Even the best Pioneering Leaders that have ever lived will have spent much of their lives as Non-Pioneering Leaders, doing ordinary things and being ordinary in many ways. 99% of people will never use Pioneering Leadership. There are no hard and fast rules; some Pioneering Leaders are attached to one big Pioneering Venture, that can sometimes represent a lifetime's work, others may flit in and out of Pioneering Leadership, using it when it makes sense to use it for them.

Try to avoid the delusion in thinking of yourself as a exclusively a Pioneering Leader if that is what you think you are. It will help you to focus on the endeavours in hand and focus on precisely when, where, how and why Pioneering Leadership is used.

Natural Pioneering Leaders Are Magnetically Attracted to Pioneering

If you are a Natural (Born) Pioneering Leader, Pioneering Leadership will come naturally to you, it will be your usual, and you'll be attracted to it like a ferrous metal to a magnet, but if you are not, making a decision to use Pioneering Leadership and become a Pioneering Leader, is a genuinely massive step to take. I don't want to understate that.

If you are not a Natural Pioneering Leader, there needs to be very good reasons to use Pioneering Leadership. The stronger, more compelling and urgent the reasons, the more sense it makes to use Pioneering Leadership. Imagine you are critically ill and about to die imminently, and you are offered Pioneering untested drugs or treatment, that might save you, but there are no guarantees. You might think that a lifeline is better than no lifeline. Imagine now, that you are the CEO of a business that is just about to fail, offered a possibility of avoiding failure and achieving extraordinary success by embracing Pioneering Leadership. You might be tempted because you have nothing left to lose. Jumping off a ship into the sea in mid-ocean is perceived by most people as suicide, but imagine the vessel was on fire, it was full of explosives, and it is only a matter of time before the explosives blow and you are toast! Jumping off the ship then doesn't seem such a bad idea. Perhaps in the explosion, debris will be scattered, some of it will float, you can climb onto it, and maybe you'll be rescued.

If I wanted to cut your arm off, you'd be understandably not happy about it, but if you were in an accident where your arm trapped you in a remote place, you might want to cut off your arm in order to stay alive, and you'd be delighted if you succeed in doing it. That might sound unbelievable, but in 2002, a lobster fisherman from Maine, Doug Goodale, cut off his own arm to survive an accident on a fishing boat, and in 2003, a climber called Aron Ralston, found himself in a hopeless situation and cut off his own arm with a penknife to survive. His incredible story was turned into a film called 127 Hours.

One reason why you might try Pioneering Leadership, is in extreme situations where Pioneering Leadership seems the least bad option. Pioneering Leadership involves adventure; meaning undertakings involving risk and uncertainty in the hope of positive outcomes. There are two primary reasons why you might want to use Pioneering Leadership:

1. Pain - The avoidance and/or alleviation of significant pain.

2. Gain – to get something you desperately want.

Pioneering Leadership is more likely to appeal to you if you are an extreme person who likes the best and most of everything, the best pain avoidance or alleviation, and the best gains, achievement, success and outcomes.

Pioneering Leadership is excellent if you are competitive and ambitious, hate being second best or worse, and If you aspire to greatness or high achievement.

Desire from either your head or your heart, to avoid or alleviate pain or to achieve significant, meaningful gain is needed to make you want to use Pioneering Leadership. It also provides you motivation and resilience to succeed using it, particularly when faced with challenges, failure or setbacks, which are almost inevitable on the journey to eventual triumph, great success and achievement.

Increase Your Consciousness and Awareness of Pioneering Leadership

If you are not aware of Pioneering Leadership you are unlikely to use it

Pioneering Leadership doesn't register on most people's top of mind awareness; they don't think to themselves should I be using Non-Pioneering Leadership or Pioneering Leadership to accomplish what I need to achieve. If you elevate your consciousness to a higher level, you will recognise that almost regardless of what you need to achieve, you have the choice of using Pioneering Leadership or Non-Pioneering Leadership.

This choice doesn't just exist at a personal level it can exist at any other level, in a business, organisation, community, country or even an international level. Given that only 100 people per month worldwide searched for Pioneering Leadership on Google at the time this book was written, it is almost inconceivable that many organisations or groups are thinking: "should we use Pioneering Leadership or Non-Pioneering Leadership". If there are only 1% of people using Pioneering Leadership, the chances are that there are even fewer organisations using it.

It is not just individuals that need a desire to use Pioneering Leadership; it is organisations and groups as well. Often in these organisations, there is collective decision-making and decision-making hierarchies, which mean that Pioneering Leadership is even less likely to be used.

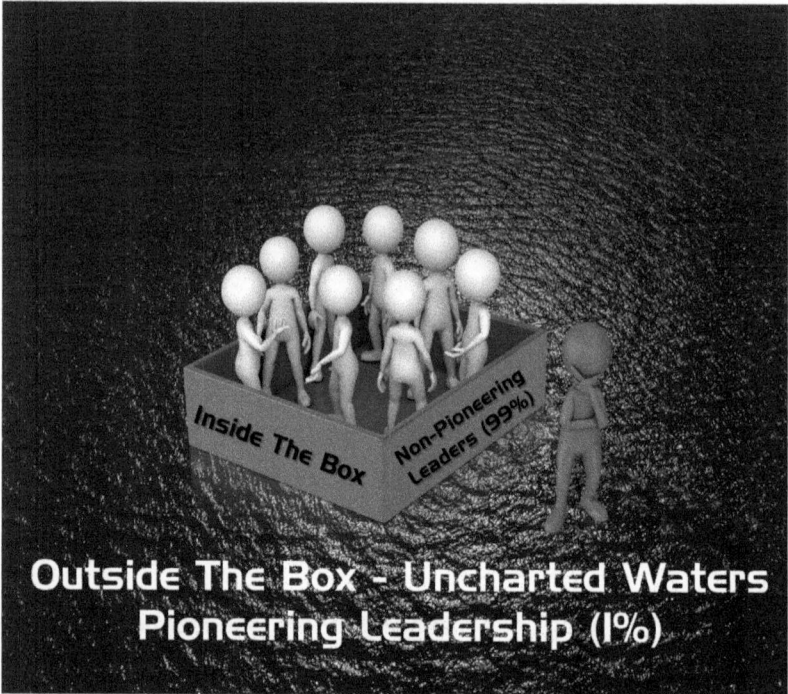

Inside The Box

Non-Pioneering Leaders (99%)

**Outside The Box - Uncharted Waters
Pioneering Leadership (1%)**

Are You Prepared to Venture Outside the Box into Uncharted Waters?

There are only two choices you can make at the highest level about how you approach anything:

1. To use Pioneering Leadership (Used by 1% of people)

2. To use Non-Pioneering Leadership (Used by 100% of people)

99% of people often won't even recognise they have a choice and will default to Non-Pioneering Leadership.

The Most Powerful Strategy on Earth

The biggest reason you might want to use Pioneering Leadership is that it is the most powerful strategy on earth, which enables you to harness infinite possibility, potential and opportunity. The reason it is these things is because it encompasses both knowledge that is the driving force of Non-Pioneering Leadership, and also infinite imagination. No lesser person than Albert Einstein, said that imagination is more important than knowledge. Imagination is the fuel for creativity and innovation. Pioneering Leadership is about more than just knowledge and imagination; it is about bringing every single factor that can be used into the mix, which enables the ultimate when it comes to new thinking, new ideas and new solutions to create a better future.

Pioneering Leadership is related to Non-Pioneering Leadership; it involves striving to be better than Non-Pioneering Leadership, going beyond today's best practice and the leading edge. However much Non-Pioneering Leadership Improves, Pioneering Leadership seeks to be even better. Pioneering Leadership is about being first, new, different and better. It is a high-level modus operandi/strategy that can be applied to any human endeavour and enterprise; its versatility is beyond equal.

Pioneering Leadership Enables you to:

1. Make the seemingly impossible possible.

2. To solve difficult problems and challenges in unique ways.

3. To create and exploit exciting opportunities.

4. Compete against tough competition and win.

5. To drive progress and move the humanity forwards.

6. To achieve extraordinary things.

8 Uses, Needs or Desires

1. To Solve Problems and Overcome Challenges.

2. To Create and Exploit Exciting Opportunities.

3. To Bring into Existence What Doesn't Exist Now.

4. To Create Improvement and Make Things Not Just Better but The Best.

5. To Drive the Most Positive Change or Transformation.

6. To Create Maximum Progress.

7. To Compete, Win and Be the Best

8. To Achieve Extraordinary Things

If Failure Is a Distinct Possibility Do You Still Want to Use Pioneering Leadership?

You need to decide if failure is a distinct possibility, do you still want to consider using Pioneering Leadership? With Pioneering Leadership, the outcomes are typically more uncertain that Non-Pioneering Leadership, but not always.

Only you can make a judgement on Risk versus Reward. With Pioneering Leadership offering an open agenda, there are usually multiple choices and options. How good you are at executing Pioneering Leadership will have a significant impact on the outcome you achieve. Nothing happens unless you make it happen, and success or failure, while possibly depending upon factors outside your control, will also depend upon your talents, skills, resources and management of elements within your control.

Can You Be Excited About Harnessing Unlimited Possibility, Potential and Opportunity?

Some people are terrified about the prospect of being able to harness unlimited possibility, potential and opportunity; others are excited and energised by the prospect.

Do You Want to Join the Greatest People Who Have Ever lived?

Joining the alumni of the Pioneering Leaders who are amongst the greatest people who have ever lived might provide you with the desire needed to use Pioneering Leadership.

Practising Pioneering Leadership gives you the opportunity to follow in the path of perhaps your greatest heroes and most admired people.

Do You Want to Make the Biggest Difference?

If you want to make the most significant difference, you can't afford to ignore Pioneering Leadership, the most powerful strategy on earth.

Do You Want to Be An Active Player in The Fourth Industrial Revolution?

"The changes are so profound that, from the perspective of human history, there has never been a time of greater promise or potential peril. My concern, however, is that decision-makers are too often caught in traditional, linear (and non-disruptive) thinking or too absorbed by immediate concerns to think strategically about the forces of disruption and innovation shaping our future." Professor Klaus Schwab, founder and executive chairman of the World Economic Forum.

Do You Want to use Pioneering Leadership?

Wanting to use Pioneering Leadership or not should be as simple as a Yes/No decision

Don't over complicate your decision making. By all means, come up with a list of pros and cons for using it and do a SWOT (Strengths, Weaknesses, Opportunities and Threats) analysis if you think it will help.

Use Pioneering Leadership for What, When and Why?

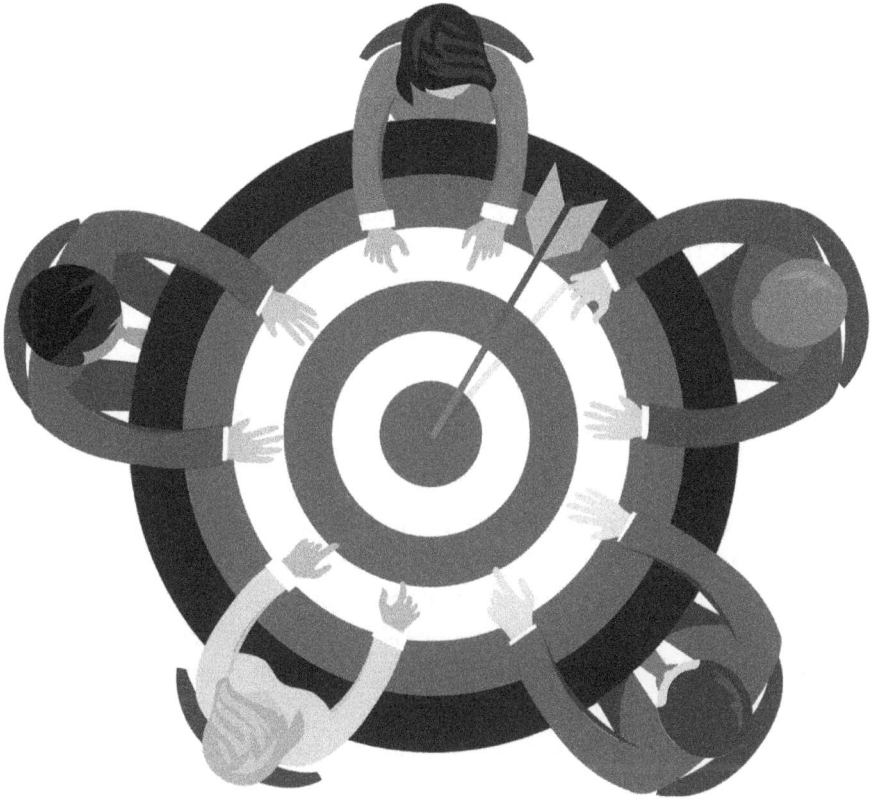

Use Pioneering Leadership When It is Best for What You Need to Accomplish

My advice is to use Pioneering Leadership when it is the best option for the endeavour or enterprise you need to accomplish, improve or create. There is a time and a place for Pioneering Leadership, and the ultimate creativity and innovation. You don't always need to reinvent the wheel.

Use it only when it is the best choice for you.

Pioneering Leadership might be something you use for a relatively small endeavour or it might become central to the success of an entire enterprise or anything in between. You might use it to solve a specific problem, as a strategy in your research and development department if you have one, or to create entire new enterprises, change or transformation that positively changes everything. Only you can decide what to use it for and when. It all depends on your situation and circumstances. Perhaps you are a sports person who wants to compete at the highest level and win; perhaps you are running a business or organisation that is right on edge in a critical situation.

I hope you will always use Pioneering Leadership for positive uses and to create a better future.

Overcome the Barriers / Obstacles Preventing You from Using It

99% of people will never use Pioneering Leadership despite it being the most powerful strategy on earth, offering the ability to harness unlimited possibility, potential and opportunity, that can enable you to make the seemingly impossible – possible, to solve difficult problems and challenges in unique ways, to create an exploit exciting opportunities, to compete against tough competition and win, to drive progress and move the human race forwards, and to achieve extraordinary things.

If you are going to be part of the 1% who uses it, the likelihood is that you'll need to overcome all the barriers and obstacles that will prevent you from using it.

If you are Natural (Born) Pioneering Leader, you will find this easier to do, but if you are naturally a Non-Pioneering Leader, it will be incredibly hard. Fear, peer pressure, ingrained habits, conditioning, doubt, uncertainty, subconscious biases, auto-responses and many more factors will work against you ever trying Pioneering Leadership. Even if you try to use it, those same things may undermine your Pioneering Leadership endeavours, which may weaken your belief that it will work for you, your resolve to make it work and your determination, resilience and tenacity to see it through and not give up, and make it through to the metaphoric finish line and glorious achievement and triumph.

First, you must get to the metaphoric Pioneering Leadership start line, and that means finding ways to overcome those barriers and obstacles, whatever they may be.

If you work for an organisation, or with others, you may well find that persuading others to go for Pioneering Leadership is the biggest challenge of all.

A bigger problem is that if you overcome those obstacles to go for Pioneering Leadership, they still have the possibility of thwarting you later. If in your heart of hearts, you don't believe in it and don't believe you can succeed using it, it is like the book "the secret" and the "law of attraction", where the universe seems to find a way of delivering what you subconsciously believe.

If you venture into the unknown, the untried and untested and do what has never been done before, or create something that didn't exist before, you don't know if it will work, or where it might end up. Temporary failure, setbacks and challenges on the journey to ultimate success and triumph are almost inevitable. It is also possible you might never succeed, but it is normally possible to extract some value, which might include lessons learnt. The first mission of the predecessor to the British Army's, legendary SAS (Special Air Service) Regiment was an unmitigated disaster; the second was a great success. When 3M first launched their Post It Note, the results were extremely disappointing. A year later they sent out free samples, and the repeat orders were incredibly high. CNN reported in 2013 that 3M was selling 50 billion

Post It Notes every year. They could have so easily been disheartened and given up before achieving success.

Next Step – Prepare For Action

The Pioneering Leadership in Uncharted Waters Framework proposes that you need to go through an initial process that involves four preparatory steps:

1. Attention – Bring Pioneering Leadership to Your Top of Mind Awareness.

2. Interest – Find Out Enough Out Pioneering Leadership to Become Interested in It.

3. Desire – Convert Interest into Desire to Use Pioneering Leadership.

4. If you get to the stage of wanting Pioneering Leadership The final step before using it is most natural one:

Prepare to Act – Make the Commitment and Move Forward to Practice Pioneering Leadership.

Chapter 9

The Core of Pioneering Leadership in Uncharted Waters™

A Lighthouse to Show You the Way to Pioneering Leadership in Uncharted Waters

Chapter 9

Metaphorically Non-Pioneering Leadership takes place on the solid ground and is built mainly on the firm foundations of knowledge and experience. Pioneering Leadership, by contrast, encompasses that same solid ground but is unconstrained by it, and involves additionally venturing into the infinite uncharted waters, which represents imagination and unlimited, possibility, potential and opportunity.

The early seafarers didn't have lighthouses to guide them and help them to avoid dangers. They didn't even have navigation charts. They had no idea what they might experience, discover and find. At times, the waters were benign and kind, and other times during storms, they were ferocious and hostile.

It must have taken immense courage to set sail beyond the horizon, not knowing whether you'd ever come back. Many did come back with tales of wonder, riches beyond belief and experiences that were beyond the comprehension of those who had stayed at home.

If you embrace Pioneering Leadership, you are metaphorically committing to leave the known and familiar and 99% of other people and "all that is inside the box" and venture forth "out the box" into Uncharted Waters in search of new things and something better.

To most people, inside the box feels safe, whereas the unknown outside the box feels unsafe.

Forgive yourself if you go through moments of doubt and anxiety; you can use fear and doubt to stay alert, stay focussed and to concentrate on what you are doing and why.

The Pioneering Leadership in Uncharted Waters Framework Core is like the star of a compass rose to provide you direction and a means of navigating out the box into the uncharted waters.

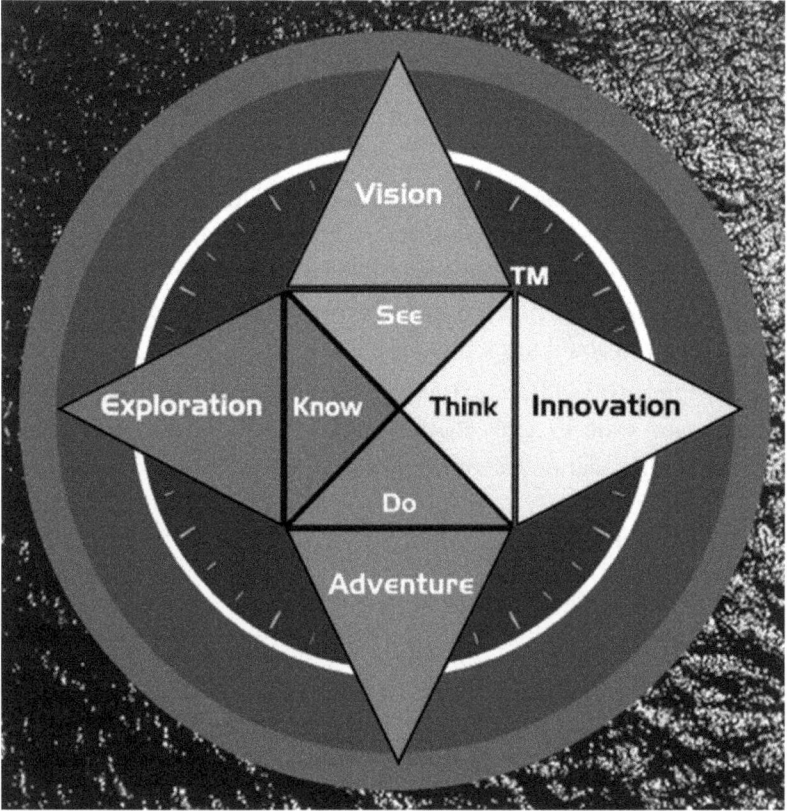

Pioneering Leadership in Uncharted Waters Core

To Practice Pioneering Leadership, You Need to Move Out the Box Into Uncharted Waters

Chapter 9

Select Your Endeavour or Enterprise

The beautiful thing about Pioneering Leadership is that it doesn't matter what your thing is, because it can be used for all endeavours and enterprises.

You can use Pioneering Leadership to help bring about world peace and harmony, to solve climate change, to alleviate poverty, hunger, malnutrition, to eradicate plastic from the oceans or toxins from the air. You could use it in any business or organisation, community or country, or you could use it in your life and career.

An enterprise will comprise multiple endeavours. It doesn't matter whether you want to apply Pioneering Leadership to an entire enterprise or a particular endeavour or both.

Find the Best Time and Situation to Use Pioneering Leadership

Choose the Best Time and Situation to Use Pioneering Leadership

Even as a staunch advocate of Pioneering Leadership, I strongly feel that there is a time and a place for Pioneering Leadership. Non-Pioneering Leadership is extremely valuable and much needed in the world. There are good reasons why Non-Pioneering Leadership, dominates the world and is used 99% of the time by 100% of people including the most talented Pioneering Leaders of all time. It is impossible, impractical and plain stupid for any individual or organisation to use Pioneering Leadership 100% of the time for everything. Pioneering Leadership could not exist without Non-Pioneering Leadership.

Nothing that I believe or say should be interpreted as being Pro Pioneering Leadership and against Non-Pioneering Leadership. There can be good and bad Pioneering Leaders and Non-Pioneering Leaders. Given that Pioneering Leaders venture into uncharted waters, where there is risk and uncertainty, it is difficult to say that a good Pioneering Leader is one who succeeds in their Pioneering endeavour or enterprise, and a bad Pioneering Leader is one who fails. It is always difficult to compare like for like, sometimes luck plays a significant part, and one must bear in mind that you've not failed until you give up. Many of the most successful Pioneering Leaders of all time, people like marine chronograph inventor John Harrison, whose accurate timepiece enabled mariners to calculate longitude, spent most of their lives working on their inventions until they eventually succeeded.

If you see Pioneering Leadership for what it is, you should know what to expect and what is possible – everything and nothing. Pioneering Leadership should evoke the spirit seen in the TV series / Films, Star Trek, in the opening sequence it says: "to boldly go where no one has gone before".

Pioneering Leadership is most suited to:

1.   A situation where progress is needed.

2.   Competitive situations.

3.   Solving Big and Important Problems that need to be solved

like: curing diseases where cures don't already exist, solving Global Warming and Environmental Issues, Creating and Maintaining Peace, Poverty, Inequality, Law and Order, Justice, Sustainable Living etc. and things like the United Nations goals.

4. Situations that involve creating a better future including better lives and careers, better communities and countries, better businesses and organisations and a better world.

5. Situations where there is a big aspiration to create and exploit worthwhile and important opportunities.

6. In situations where what you have been doing either hasn't been working at all or hasn't been working as well as you'd like.

Use pioneering Leadership when you want to use the most powerful strategy on earth, to unlock unlimited potential, possibility and opportunity and to:

1. Make the seemingly impossible possible.

2. Solve difficult problems in unique ways.

3. Create and exploit exciting opportunities.

4. Compete against tough competition and win.

5. Drive progress and move the human race forward.

6. Achieve extraordinary things.

7. Change the Game.

8. Break the Mould.

9. Blaze a Trail.

10. Disrupt.

There are no limits to the number of applications for Pioneering Leadership. You have to decide when you think it is best to use it. It can be used for the smallest things or the biggest things. Often it is used out of laziness; why put in more effort to achieve an outcome that you have to? I remember while still at school, having a part-time job with the once famous British retail company, British Home Stores. I used to work on Saturdays in the menswear department. Before Sunday trading was allowed in the UK, most retail stores were closed on Sundays. One Sunday, my friend and I, who were the only two part-time men employed in the all-female store, were asked if we could work on Sunday. There were rules about needing three people in the store and an engineer had to go in and do some vital maintenance work, so we were invited in to make up the numbers. They had an idea that we could spend the whole day cleaning fluff out the ventilation grills in the ceiling. We were given some tall ladders and a paintbrush, to painstakingly prize the fluff out of each of the many tiny grill holes on grills throughout the store. Once the engineer was gone, which happened quickly, we were the only ones left in the store. We had another idea. First we tried to vacuum clean the grills which didn't work, we then had another idea which did; we used a giant broom to sweep the grills on the ceiling effectively. Clouds of dust and fluff fell out making a real mess, which we quickly vacuumed up, and in a relatively short time, we'd done our allotted work for the day. There was no one to talk to, no numbers to call, we just had to wait until the time at the end of the day when we'd be let out.

Our attention then turned to what we could do to amuse ourselves for a whole day in a giant department store; we explored the areas where we weren't usually allowed to go. In the toy department, they had radio-controlled cars, and we raced some of them around the empty aisles, which was great fun. The store was delighted with the finished result; they couldn't believe we'd finished all the grills, they never expected us to do as many as we did.

Use Pioneering Leadership Here

It Takes Judgement and Experience to Find the Best Place/ Situation to Use Pioneering Leadership

Think about using Pioneering Leadership in any situation where there is a need for new thinking, new ideas and new solutions, improvement, change or transformation. Use Pioneering Leadership when you want to be ahead of the game, not behind the game, and for any situations where the following are beneficial including:

1. Reinvention

2. Renewal

3. Transformation etc.

Pioneering Leadership is the best thing to use when you want to achieve the very best results and outcomes; you just need to reconcile that desire, with the truth that with Pioneering Leadership involves risk and uncertainty in the hope of positive outcomes, but outcomes are unknown, and success can rarely be guaranteed. That is the Achilles Heel of Pioneering Leadership.

You could argue that Pioneering Leadership is High Risk – High Reward and that Non-Pioneering Leadership is Lower Risk – Lower Reward, but, often the reverse is true; remaining anchored to the past, sticking with the tried and tested in a fast-moving world can sometimes be the highest risk of all. Giant corporations are at highest risk of this; they have a considerable amount to lose and continually risk disruption by small upstarts and a changing world, which is why the lifespan of S&P 500 companies has fallen so much.

Just remember Pioneering Leaders are usually the ones with "balls" meaning "real courage". Look at Elon Musk today and you'll see someone trying to make a massive difference and achieve extraordinary things. To achieve big, you have to think big, and be prepared to act big. There are few better examples of this than Malcolm Stamper, who was in 1966 tasked by the CEO of aircraft company Boeing, to build the biggest aircraft in the world, which became known as the 747 – Jumbo Jet. Stamper led a team of 50,000 people to achieve the task, building the world's largest factory. The entire future of Boeing depended upon the success of the project. His obituary stated: "The 747 was an engineering and management challenge as monumental as the cavernous 400-seat plane". It was to become a resounding success, but it was not without its challenges; during the 1969 / 70 recession, the company had to lay off two-thirds of its 101,000 employees. It established Boeing as the world's leading aircraft manufacturer and gave it a market dominance that lasted decades.

Pioneering Leadership does not suit risk-averse people who like to pussyfoot around.

Deciding to use Pioneering Leadership can be a small insignificant decision, but it can also be the biggest decision that you are likely to take in your career or your life. If your decision to use Pioneering Leadership is a big one, its ramifications both positive and negative can be huge. In many ways, the bigger the consequences, the more committed you are likely to be to the desired outcome and the greater the chance will be of achieving it. If you decide to use Pioneering Leadership, do so, eyes wide open, with the full knowledge or at least anticipation of the adventure that lies before you. It is often better to measure twice and cut once. I'll usually go through a Pioneering Leadership journey mentally before I commit to doing it in real life. It is amazing how doing that, makes you think of the pitfalls, anticipate potential problems and mistakes and avoid or mitigate them as best you can. Good ideas often take considerable time to evolve and be developed. I remember going on a training course early in my career, where I was taught the lesson of the six P's (Prior Planning and Preparation Prevents Poor Performance". Of course, no amount of planning and preparation can prepare you for every situation, particularly a Pioneering one, that by definition involves risk and uncertainty.

Understand - Out the Box – Meaning and Significance

A Box is a Metaphor for an Endeavour or Enterprise. Non-Pioneering Leadership is in the box and Pioneering Leadership is outside the box in metaphoric uncharted waters.

A sealed box is a metaphor for a building block. Being a block makes it easy to identify and by the block being hollow i.e. taking the form of a box, you can imagine that the box encapsulates and provides boundaries/limits, within which the content can be stored.

Most people are familiar with one of the three phrases, which have the same meaning: Out the box, Outside the Box, or Out the Square. Additionally, most people associate these phrases with thinking, e.g. Think Out The box, Think Outside The Box and Think Outside The Square.

> "Thinking Outside the Box is a metaphor that means to think differently, unconventionally, or from a new perspective. This phrase often refers to novel or creative thinking. The term is thought to derive from management consultants in the 1970s and 1980s challenging their clients to solve the "nine dots" puzzle, whose solution requires some lateral thinking." Wikipedia

Pioneering Leadership isn't just about thinking, it is also about seeing, knowing and doing differently to create a better future, better lives and careers, better businesses and organisations, better communities and countries and a better world.

The Box Objectives and Cause and Effect

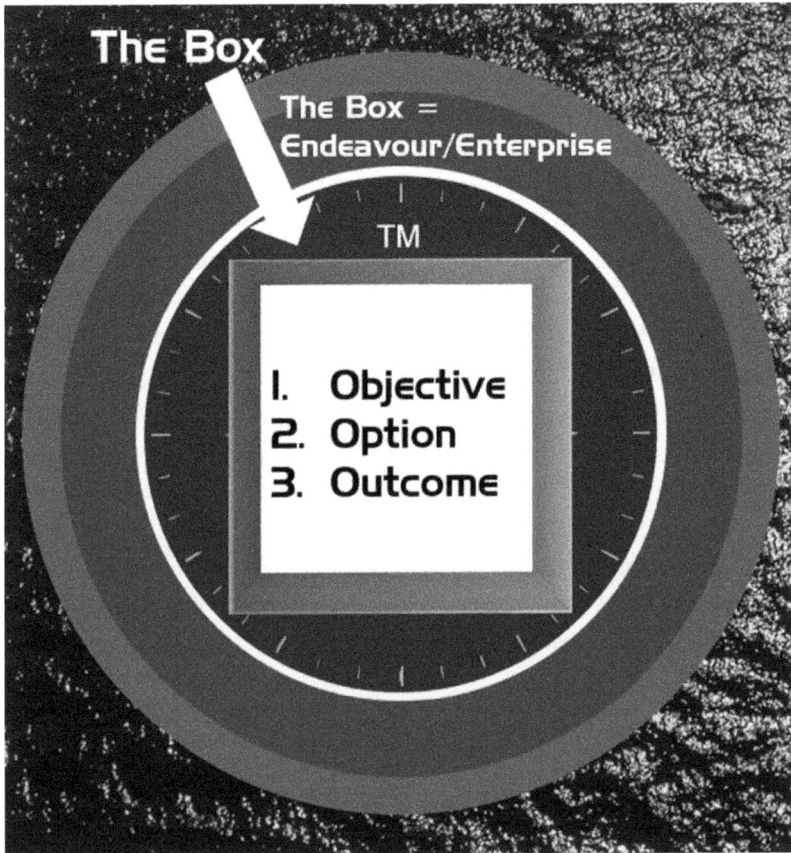

At the highest-level Pioneering Leadership is about just three things:

1. The Objective – Definition of what you want. (This becomes the box / label)

2. The Options – What can be used to get what you want.

3. Outcomes – What you actually get.

Chapter 9

Every endeavour/enterprise has an objective or goal, which is a desire, purpose and reason for being. There are usually multiple different options for the way in which the objective/goal can be achieved. Some options are better than others. Some people or organisations will be able to achieve objectives better than others. If the objective of an endeavour was to win a sports competition, multiple people/teams would compete against each other and there would be a winner and losers. If the objective is to win and the outcome is that you do win, then you've achieved your objective. If you didn't win, next time you might think about what you could do better (Options) so that you could win next time. Pioneering Leadership might involve doing what has been done before but better, or it might involve doing or creating something that doesn't yet exist. Options are the cause and outcomes are the effect.

In the 2018 Formula One motor racing series, Mercedes Team Boss, Toto Wolff, said " We are just not giving up. This is not a championship we are going to lose. We need to understand why we have been out-performed. So it is development, research, analysis, mindset, work ethic, fun." Pioneering Leadership can involve putting everything on the table that can impact the outcome. Toto suggested many options , but the only limits to the possible options are the limits to your imagination.

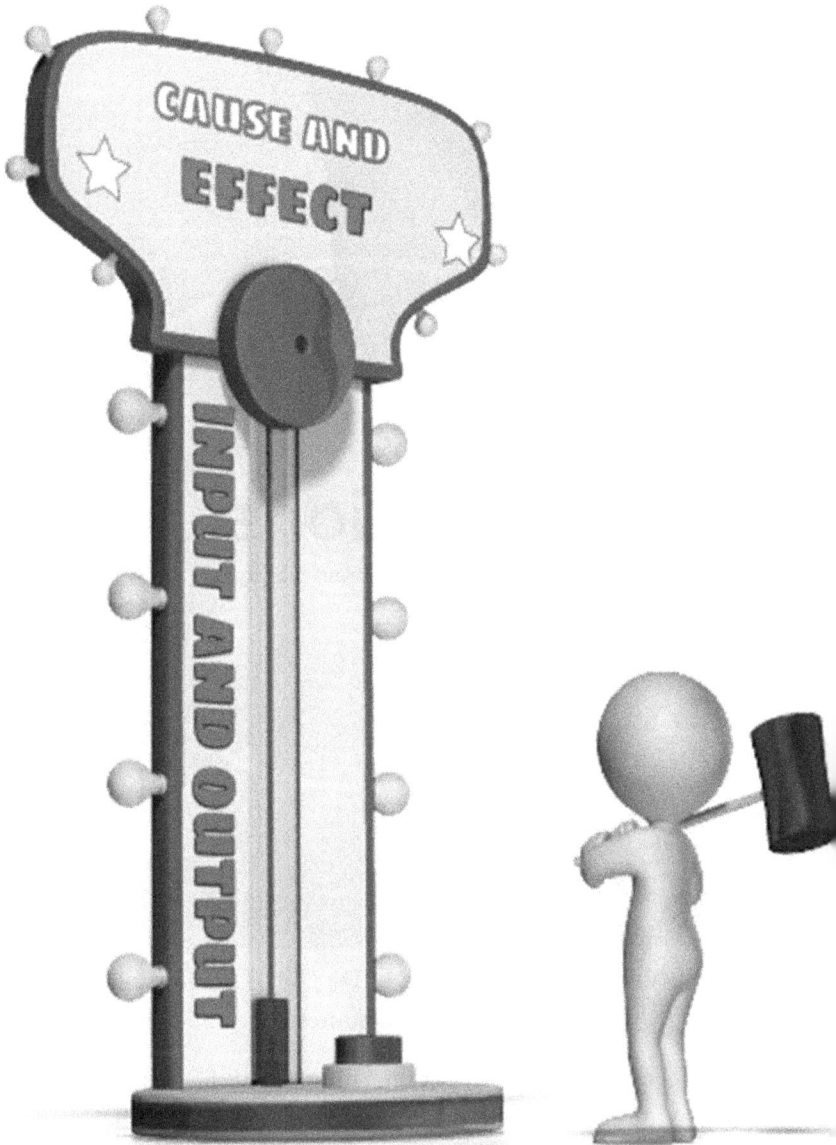

Options are the Cause and Outcomes are the Effect.

Change Your Input to Get a Different Output

The Box Options

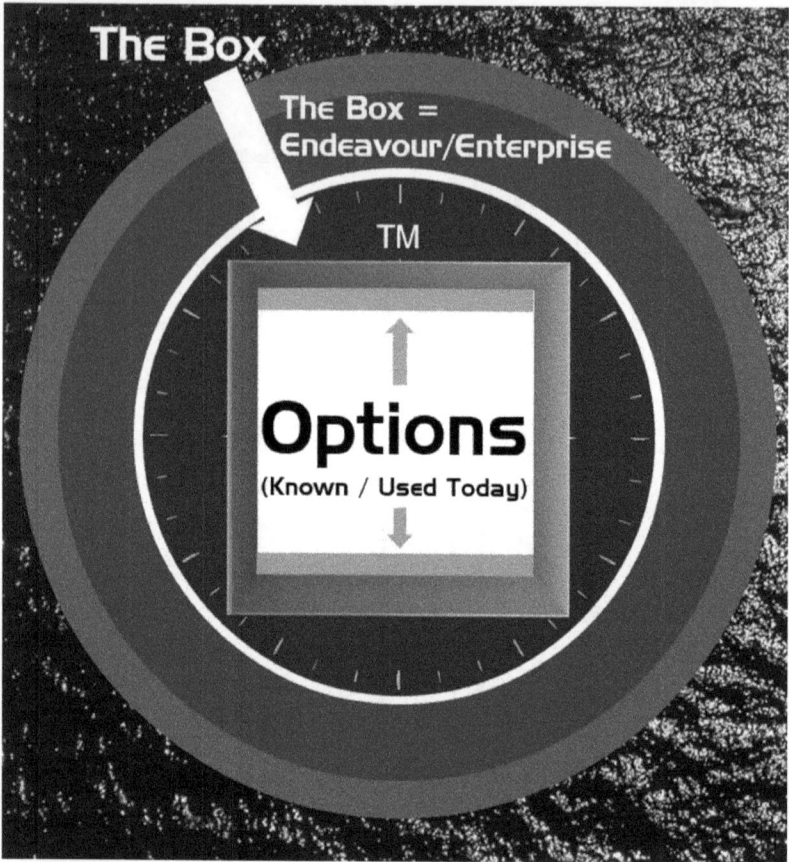

The Box

The Box =
Endeavour/Enterprise

TM

Options
(Known / Used Today)

Options Are What You Can / Do Use to Achieve the Desired Outcomes

The top of the box marks the boundary of the first option you can use, and the bottom of the box marks the boundary of the last known option you can use. These options inside the box, represent the status quo and the options available today used by both Non-Pioneering Leaders and other Pioneering Leaders.

Pioneering Leaders seek to create better outcomes than the best outcomes that others are achieving (best practice) and therefore try to discover and use, new, different and better options, which enable them to do so.

The Box Outcomes

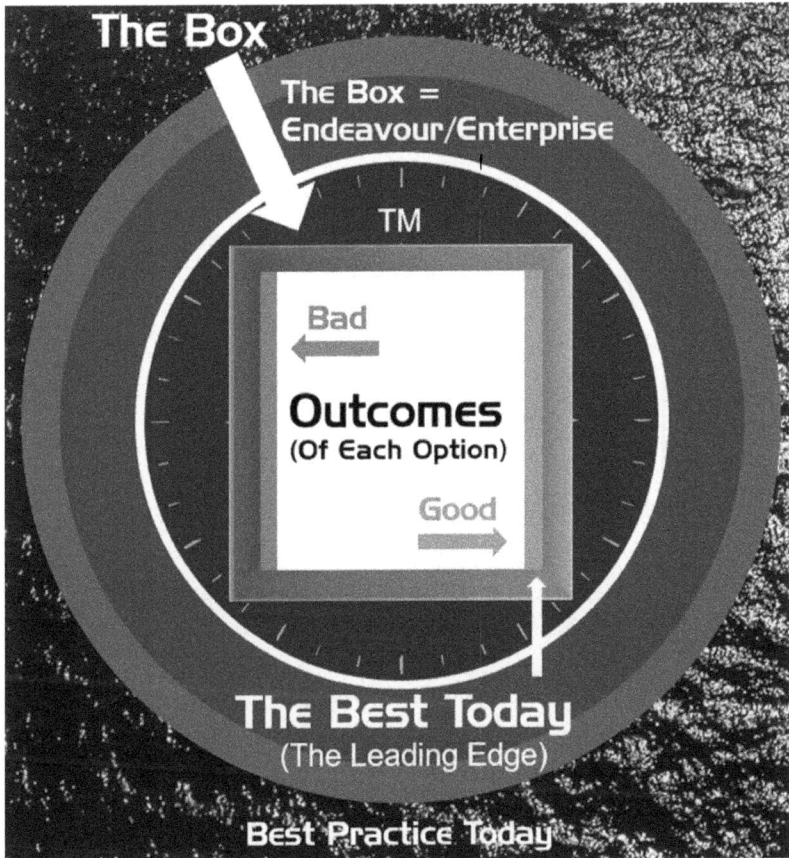

Some Options Will Be Good Others Bad and One Will Be the Best

The left side of the box represents the worst limit of the outcome.

The right side of the box represents the best outcome, which also could be seen as "The Leading Edge."

The box represents the status quo / business as usual, and what is practised by Non-Pioneering Leaders. Some options will produce better outcomes than others.

Non-Pioneering Leaders are Usually Pleased to Be as Good as The Best – Pioneering Leaders Aren't

Pioneering Leaders look to the leading edge of anything as a starting point, they desire to be the best and find new, different and better ways or to create things that don't yet exist.

A Non-Pioneering Leader will study how best to do things and will typically follow the rules and take a similar approach to others. They will go on courses, learn from experts, benchmark and strive to achieve best practice in all that they do. The Pioneering Leader might study and benchmark also, but their aspirations are higher. They may challenge and question everything and won't be afraid to try new things and come up with new options to create better outcomes.

The Pioneering Leadership Formula

Pioneering Leaders Create New Objectives, New Options and New Outcomes That Are Better

In the simplest terms Pioneering Leadership is just about 3 variables that converted into a formula is:

Objective + Option = Outcome – (Pioneering Leaders are Interested in the Best Outcomes.)

You can start with any of the three variables, e.g.

1. Start with an Objective

2. Start with an Option

3. Start with an Outcome

Start with an Objective

Starting with an objective is by far the most common and used approach. You know what you want to achieve at the start, and your desire is to discover the best option that will deliver the best outcome.

Start with an Option

When trying to develop a super strong adhesive, the company 3M accidentally discovered a low-tack pressure-sensitive adhesive. They were not looking to develop this; they had no objective to develop it, and no idea of what they could use it for and what outcome they could achieve.

Start with an Outcome

In 1945 Percy Spencer, an engineer working for the electronics company Raytheon noticed that while he was working on microwave radar, a chocolate bar in his pocket started to melt. This is how the microwave oven was invented.

Pioneering Leaders Seek to Drive Progress for Themselves and Others and End With?

Pioneering Leaders drive progress and seek to end with:

1. Better Objectives.

2. Better Options.

3. Better Outcomes.

See Options as a Chef See's a Recipe, Ingredients and Cooking Techniques

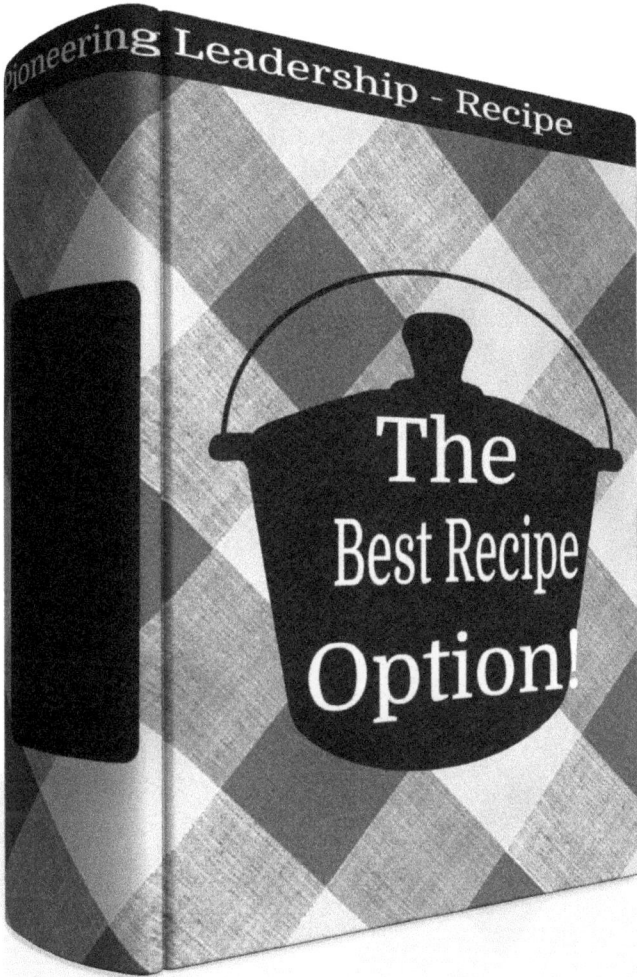

See Options as a Chef Sees a Recipe, Ingredients and Cooking Techniques

Chapter 9

You would have thought that there would be no more need today for new recipes or cookbooks, yet each year new ones appear.

When thinking of Pioneering New Options, you need to think about all the ingredients that could help you to achieve your goals; stock your Pioneering Leadership larder with all of them and get as creative as you can be. Invariably it is a combination of factors that come together to create success. Top sports people, for example, might discover that their success comes from more than their sporting skills. Things like psychology, fitness, diet, hydration, exercise regime, environment, clothing and equipment, climate and altitude, happiness, teamwork, coaching, relaxation, motivation, preparation, sleep, friendship, support, self-belief, supplements, weight and countless other factors could all impact their success.

Pioneering Leadership Interrelated with Non-Pioneering Leadership

Pioneering Leadership is interrelated with Non-Pioneering Leadership.

In 1946, Broadway Musical, Annie Get Your Gun, which was composed by Irving Berlin, there was a song called "Anything You Can Do (I can do better)" "The song is a duet, with one male singer and one female singer attempting to outdo each other in increasingly complex tasks". Wikipedia. This song reflects the relationship between Pioneering Leadership and Non-Pioneering Leadership.

Pioneering Leadership wants to be better than Non-Pioneering Leadership. However much Non-Pioneering Leadership achieves, Pioneering Leadership wants to be better. It doesn't matter how much Non-Pioneering Leadership achieves or improves, Pioneering Leadership always wants to be better and frequently achieves its objective. I am sure you can imagine that it is frustrating for Non-Pioneering Leadership, continually relegated to second place, whatever they do.

The only time that this doesn't happen is when Pioneering Leadership creates something completely new, where Non-Pioneering Leadership isn't even in the game.

In the business world, big established Non-Pioneering Leader companies can be disrupted by small Pioneering-Leader start-ups. The small Pioneering Leader start-up can become the next big established company and can easily become static, arrogant and complacent, and without realising it, they can then become the Non-Pioneering Leader only to themselves be disrupted by another Pioneering Leader company.

Given that there is only one Pioneering Leader for every 99 Non-Pioneering Leaders, most are not visible, operating under the radar, until they become a threat, even then, they are often dismissed as not a real threat, often until it is too late.

Pioneering Leadership outcomes eventually becomes the new normal; as it starts to be used by others, it becomes Non-Pioneering Leadership. When Henry Ford introduced the production line, it was Pioneering Leadership, now everyone uses it, and it is Non-Pioneering. The benefits of Pioneering Leadership fade over time, but if you've grown from nothing to the size Facebook was after ten years, you'll have done well. Many Pioneering Companies don't just have a long list of Pioneering products and services behind them, many have been in entirely different industries. We know Nokia as a Finnish multinational telecommunications, information technology, and consumer electronics company. What most people don't know is that its origins go back to 1865 since which time it has been in the pulp mill, electricity generation and rubber industries. Some Pioneering Leadership offers only short-term benefits, while others can have very long-term benefits.

Pioneering Leadership is competitive and doesn't just want to be better; it wants to be the best, new different and original. It aspires to transformation, not just change and to the ultimate in revolution as well as the ultimate in evolution. Pioneering Leadership may not always succeed in its quest, but with its attitude and relentless drive for progress, advancement and betterment, it is a formidable foe that ultimately comes out on top. If you think of a military analogy, it may sometimes lose battles, but invariably it wins wars. Some Pioneering Leaders will fail, but others will succeed, and when they do, the results are usually extraordinary not ordinary.

Being Outnumbered Pioneering Leaders Sometimes Struggle with Non-Pioneering Leaders

4 Metaphors (Ways) to Get Out the Box

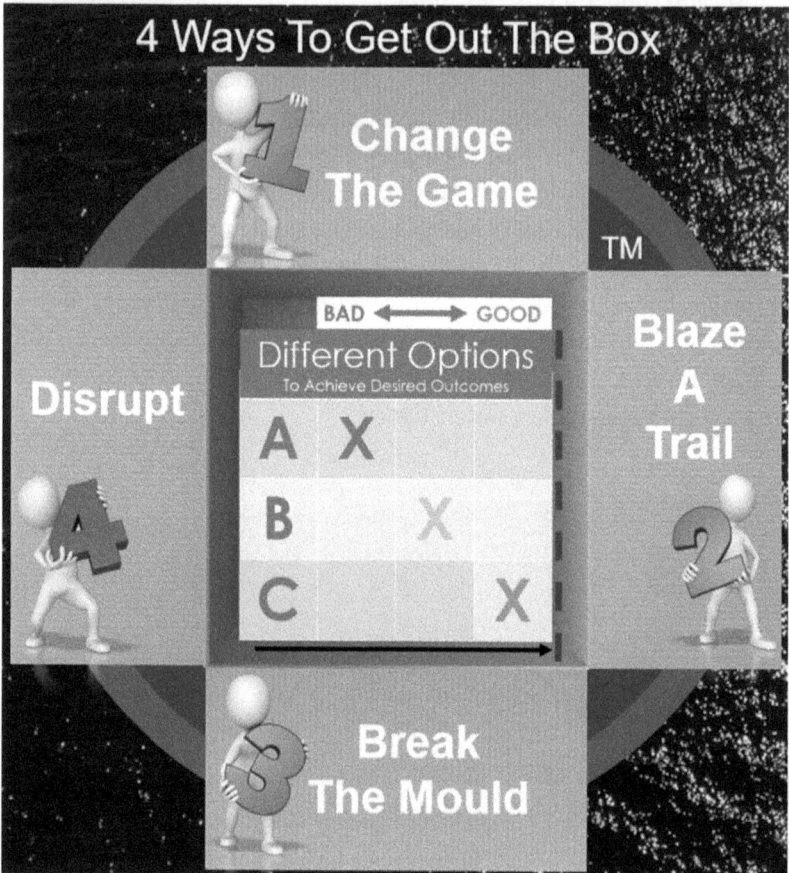

Metaphors are The Best Way of Understanding Pioneering Leadership

When trying to learn any new concept or theory, it is easy to think in abstract terms, detached from the real world and your situation. Metaphors are the best way of understanding Pioneering Leadership. Most people instinctively understand "out the box thinking", yet what the box is and represents isn't so clear.

The Pioneering Leadership in Uncharted Waters Framework uses a box to represent any endeavour or enterprise and uses the sides of the box to represent the constraints of the options that currently exist (as the top/bottom limits), with the (left / right) sides representing good and bad outcomes corresponding to each option. The best outcome today is on the bottom right position of the box, when the options are ranked from worst to best.

Pioneering Leadership involves venturing into the uncharted waters of infinite possibility, potential and opportunity that lie outside the box.

Four metaphors perfectly position Pioneering Leadership, because they are widely recognised, they are:

1. Change the Game.

2. Blaze a Trail.

3. Break the Mould.

4. Disrupt.

While these terms are often used interchangeably; different people often interpret them differently. Each interpretation that anyone has ever given me seems to apply to Pioneering Leadership.

If you evoke your interpretations of these metaphors, there is an excellent chance it will lead you to Pioneering Leadership.

"If you change the way you look at things, the things you look at change".

Dr Wayne Dyer

4 Things You Need to Change to Break Out the Box

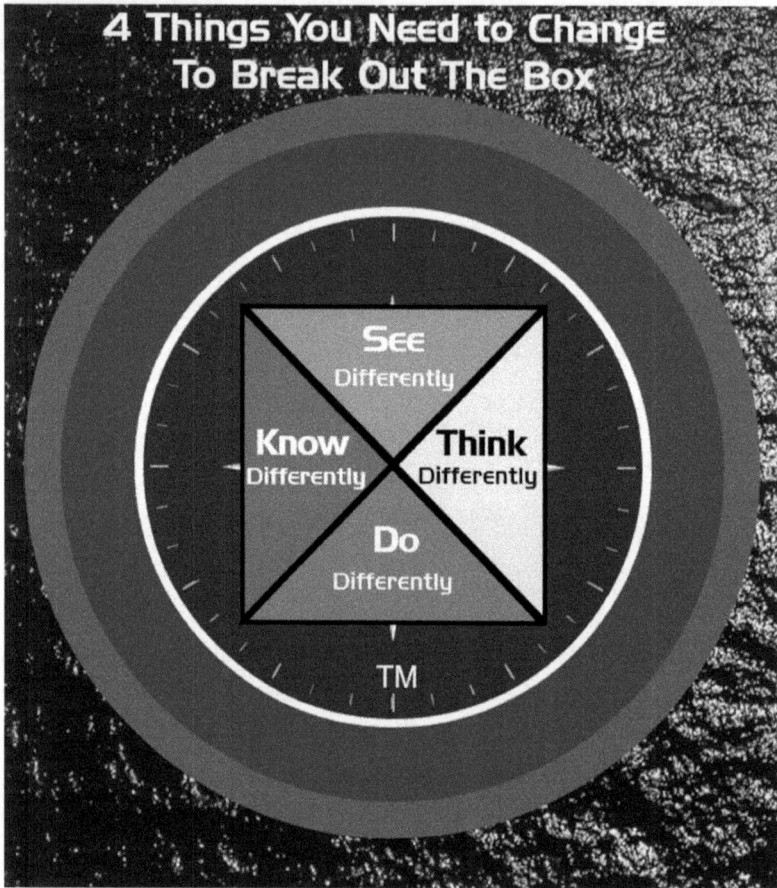

The 4 Things You Need to Change to Break Out the Box – The Way You See, Think, Know and Act

Non-Pioneering Leadership is "Business as Usual", it is what 100% of people do 99% of the time. Pioneering Leadership is the opposite of "Business as Usual" it is what 1% or less of people do sometimes. Non-Pioneering Leadership is "Ordinary", Pioneering Leadership seeks to be "Extraordinary". Non-Pioneering Leadership is "In the box", Pioneering Leadership involves venturing "Out the box" into the unknown, and infinite possibility, potential and opportunity.

To enable you to practice Pioneering Leadership, you need to strive to be different from Non-Pioneering Leadership and the way that you do this is to change four things:

1. Change What You See and How You See Things.

2. Change What and How You Think.

3. Change What You Know.

4. Change What You Do.

Changing these things, particularly if you a natural Non-Pioneering Leader is not easy, and often takes practice and sometimes some help to get you started.

Change What You See and How You See Things

There are four easy ways you can change how you see things:

1. Try to see the big picture, taking a helicopter view.

2. Go into the minutiae, put things under a metaphoric microscope to see the detail.

3. Put yourself in the metaphoric shoes of others and see things from other's perspective.

4. Look back to the past and learn lessons from hindsight and use that and your knowledge and experience to develop foresight and anticipate the future in a way that others don't.

5. Make a paradigm shift and change your perception of things.

Chapter 9

Change What and How You Think

1. Develop creative thinking.

2. Look for and identify the connection between things that others don't normally connect.

3. Try to think laterally.

4. Brainstorm and seek to start your creativity working.

5. Take a pen and paper to bed and carry it around during the day and whey you think of something write it down, so you can remember it and refer to it later.

6. Open your mind to new possibilities, opportunities and potential contained within things.

7. Think up original new ideas, that can make a difference.

8. Using knowledge, develop new hypotheses you can try and test.

Change What You Know and How You Interpret Your Knowledge

1. Increase your knowledge in relevant areas.

2. Question and challenge everything.

3. Analyse things and look for patterns.

4. Become observant and curious and ask yourself questions continuously.

5. Apply meaning to knowledge.

Change What You Do and How You Act

Action is everything, it doesn't matter how clever and knowledgeable you are, how creative and out the box your thinking if you don't translate it all into action that delivers results. There is a saying that is often misattributed to Einstein: "insanity is continuing to do the same things and expecting a different result.". This might be true, but against that argument is the truth that sometimes persistence pays. Remember that Pioneering Leadership is about taking the different path to others. What others do may change frequently, so you need to be highly agile and able to change as others change, to be ahead and stay ahead.

"Dare to be different and choose to make a difference."

Pioneering Leadership in Uncharted Waters Framework Core

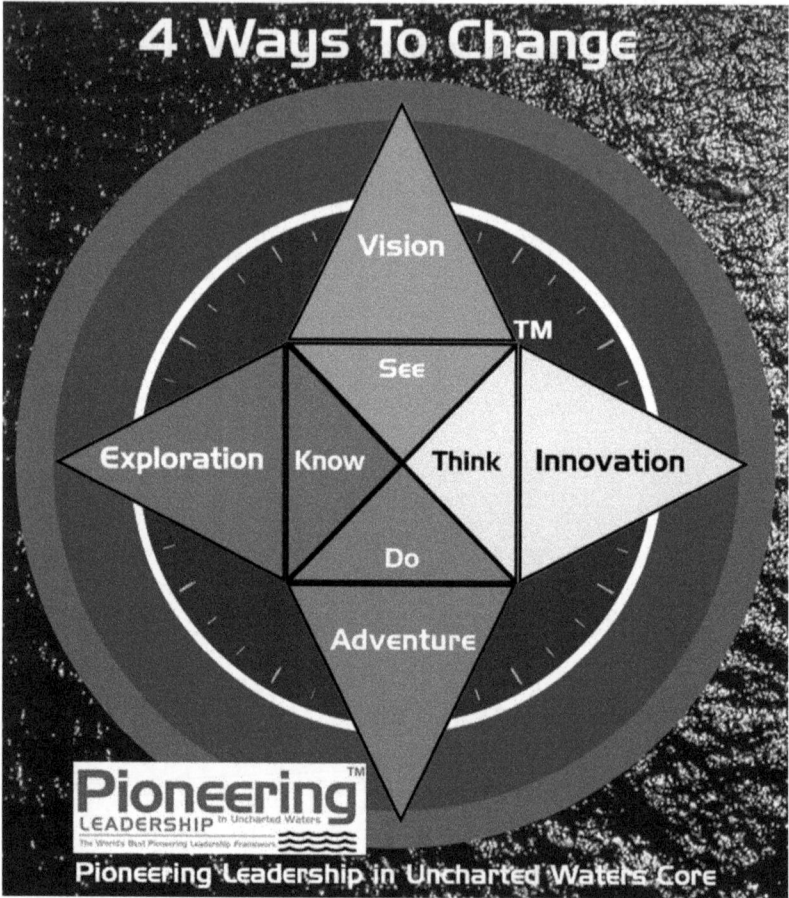

The Core of the Pioneering in Uncharted Waters Framework

Vision
Foresight

Innovation
Ideas

Adventure
Action

Exploration
Curiosity

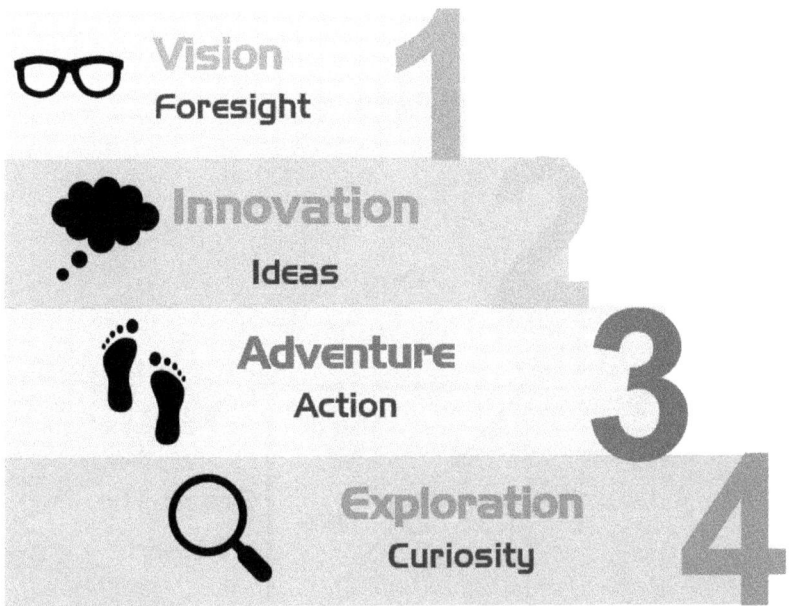

The exciting news is that to become a Pioneering Leader, you get to become a Visionary, Innovator, Adventurer and Explorer.

You need to learn, practice and improve the four principal elements of Pioneering Leadership:

1. Vision

2. Innovation

3. Adventure

4. Exploration

Chapter 9

Flip Side

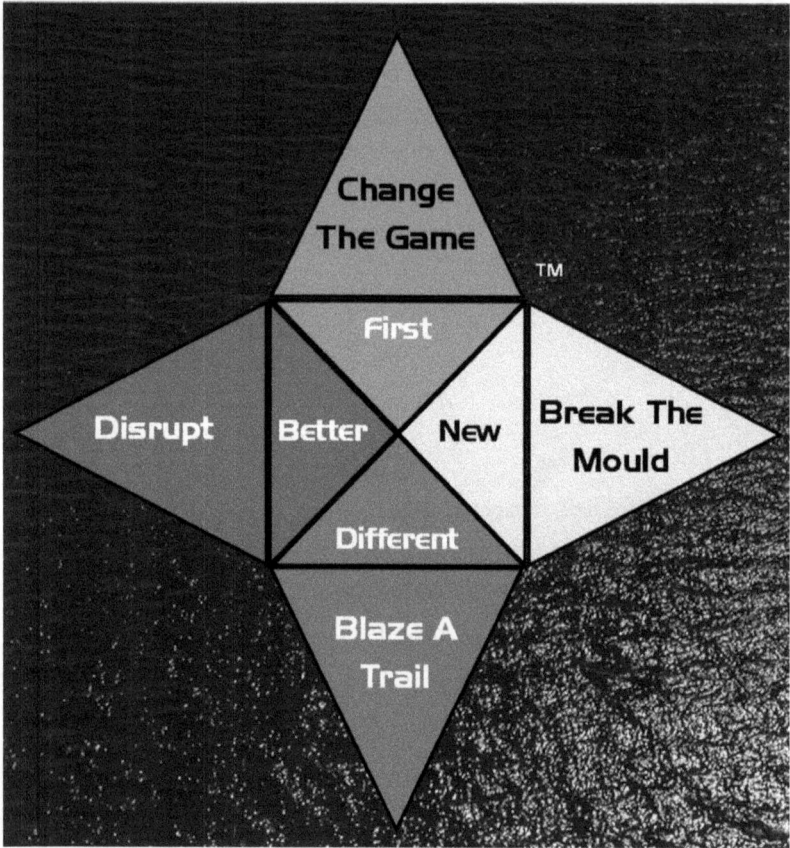

The Flip Side of the Pioneering Leadership in Uncharted Waters Core

To break out the box and change the game, break the mould, blaze a trail and disrupt, you need to prepare to venture into uncharted waters by thinking about being:

1. First.

2.   New.

3.   Different.

4.   Better.

When people think about Pioneering Leadership, they often think of Revolutionary Progress, but Pioneering Leadership could involve either Revolutionary Progress or Evolutionary Progress. Sometimes the smallest pioneering things can make the biggest difference.

Vision

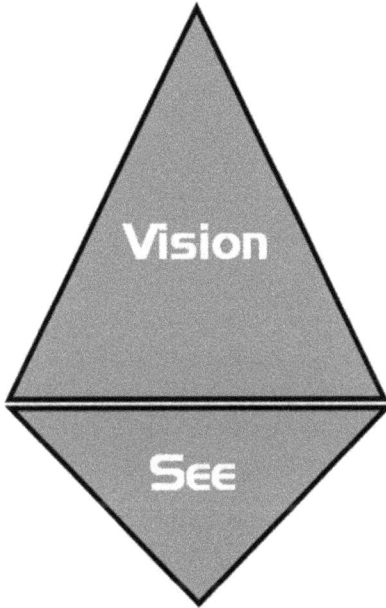

Foresight

"Dream and see what could be and what should be in the future and see things in new ways."

Vision
Foresight

When you are running a business, there is a constant need to reinvent oneself. One should have the foresight to stay ahead in times of rapid change and rid ourselves of stickiness in any form in the business. Shiv Nadar (Indian billionaire industrialist and philanthropist).

1. Develop Foresight.

2. See What Is?

3. See What Could Be?

4. See What Should Be?

5. See What Is Going to be?

6. See Things from New Perspectives?

"My experience in life has taught me that the only people who achieve on a grand scale are those who dream on a grand scale." Dame Stephanie Shirley"

Innovation

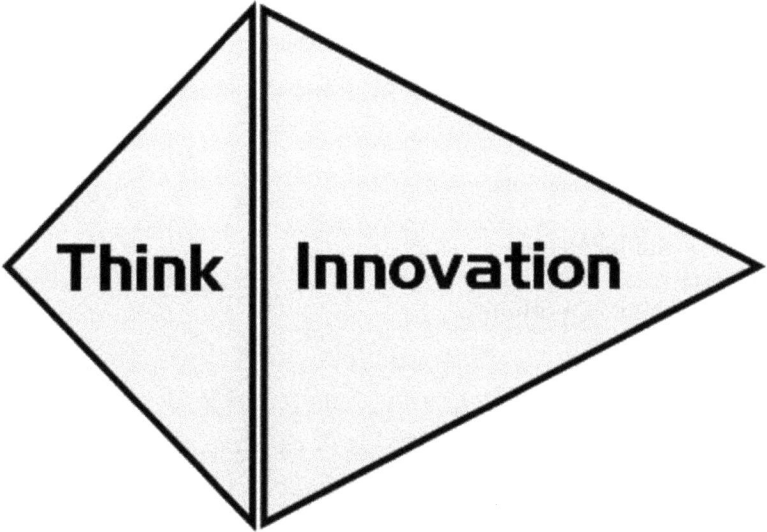

Ideas

*"Imagination and creativity: New Thinking, New Ideas,
New Solutions, New Things in New Ways".*

Chapter 9

"Imagination is more important than knowledge. For knowledge is limited, whereas imagination embraces the entire world, stimulating progress, giving birth to evolution."
Albert Einstein

1. Develop Ideas.

2. Think Possibility.

3. Think Potential.

4. Think Opportunity.

"Be less curious about people and more curious about ideas". Marie Curie (Polish and naturalized-French physicist /scientist, who conducted pioneering research on radioactivity).

"Believe in something. Even if it means sacrificing everything". Nike

Adventure

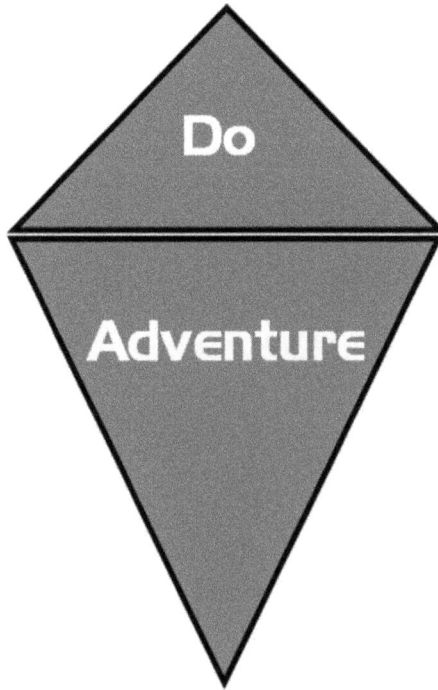

Action

"An undertaking involving risk and uncertainty in the hope of positive outcomes with the expectation of excitement and reward".

Adventure
Action

3

1. Take Action.

2. Take Risks.

3. Face Uncertainty.

4. Expect Positive Things.

Adventure is worthwhile in itself".

Adventure is worthwhile in itself". Amelia Earhart
(American Aviation Pioneer)

Exploration

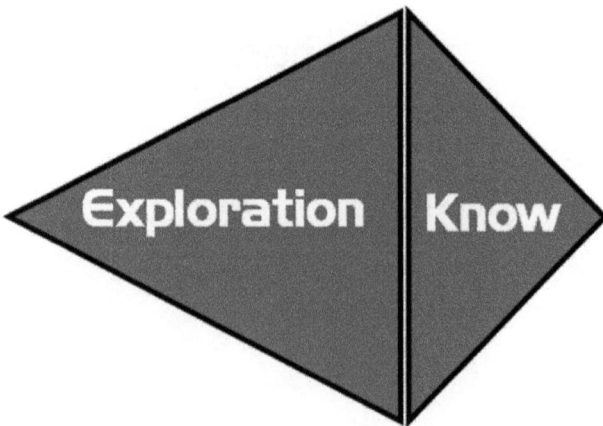

Curiosity

"A journey to make discoveries to find possibilities, opportunities, meaning, answers and the truth".

Q **Exploration**
Curiosity
4

1. Develop Curiosity

2. Discover Facts

3. Question

4. Interpret

"Exploration is the engine that drives innovation. Innovation drives economic growth". Edith Widder (American scientist, oceanographer, marine biologist, and the Co-founder, CEO and Senior Scientist at the Ocean Research & Conservation Association).

Sequence

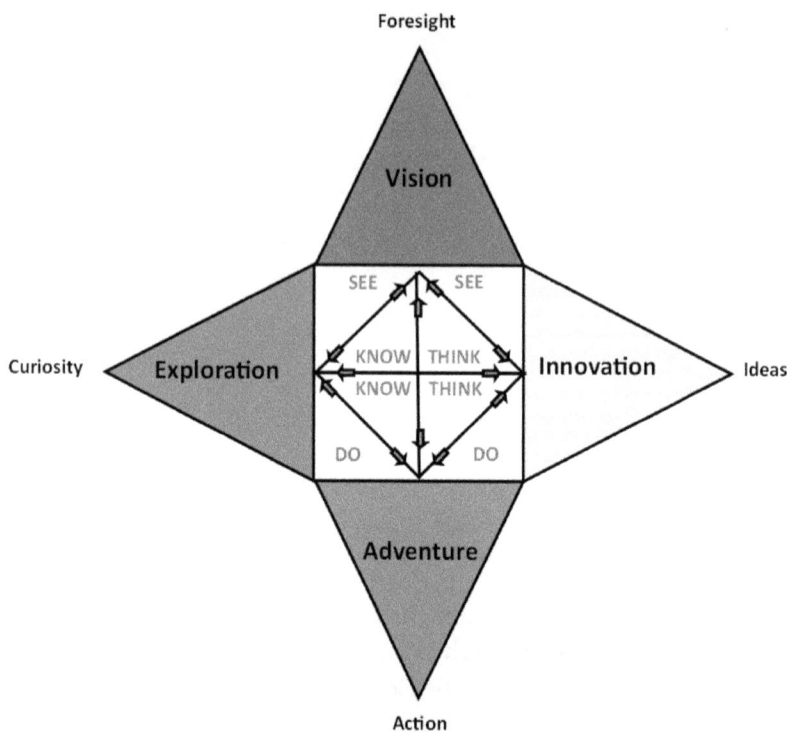

Knowing Where to Start the Pioneering Leadership in Uncharted
Waters Framework is Not Easy

When asked where you should start with the Pioneering Leadership in Uncharted Waters Framework Core, the answer depends upon
your circumstances that I don't know. The truth is that you can start
anywhere:

1. Start with a problem.

2. Start with a desire.

3. Start with seeing an opportunity.

4. Start with an outcome or situation.

5. Start with curiosity.

6. Start with an idea.

7. Start with a vision.

8. Start by doing something.

All the elements of the Pioneering Leadership in Uncharted Waters Framework are connected, related and interrelated. The important thing is to understand the different elements and work with them all as you feel you need to. You might be able to go straight from an idea to action and quickly achieve the outcome you desire, or you may need to spend a long time in exploration or innovation or developing a vision. Pioneering Leadership is a creative process, that requires you to be creative.

We are so used to being spoon fed step by step solutions with the promise of guaranteed results if they are followed, that is can be a shock to in effect be given a set of principles and a framework to work with, and a blank piece of paper.

Nothing is likely to happen unless you recognise the difference between Pioneering Leadership and Non-Pioneering Leadership and make a conscious choice to use Pioneering Leadership for a specific purpose or situation.

You might use it for the tiniest task that is over in a moment, through to using it for big enterprises and endeavours like setting up a new Pioneering Business or disrupting an entire market, or in science on a quest to make discoveries that take a lifetime to achieve like eradicating all disease.

Learn and Do

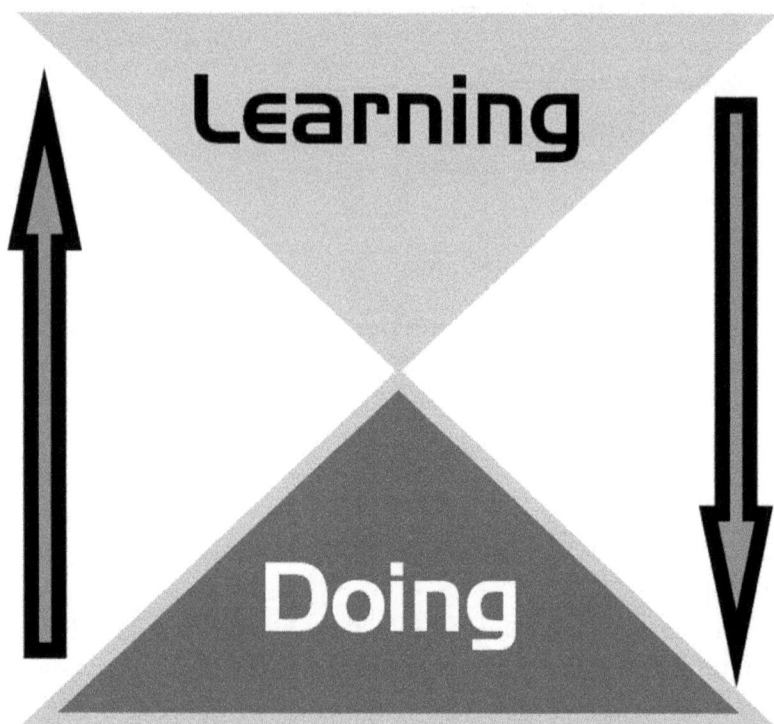

To practice Pioneering Leadership, you need to learn about it and then just do it, but doing it should be a continual journey of learning, which shapes what you do and sometimes takes you in new directions. By doing, you gain experience, and experience leads to insights and wisdom. The more you learn, the more you will sometimes discover you don't know, and the more you realise there is to learn. The most successful Pioneering Leaders are usually on a continual cycle of learning and doing that never ends. However good you get, you can always be better.

Pioneering Leaders need to keep an open mind and an open agenda; you won't always know where you are likely to end up and where the Pioneering Leadership journey may take you, or indeed when the journey should end.

Next Steps

Go Deeper – Go Further

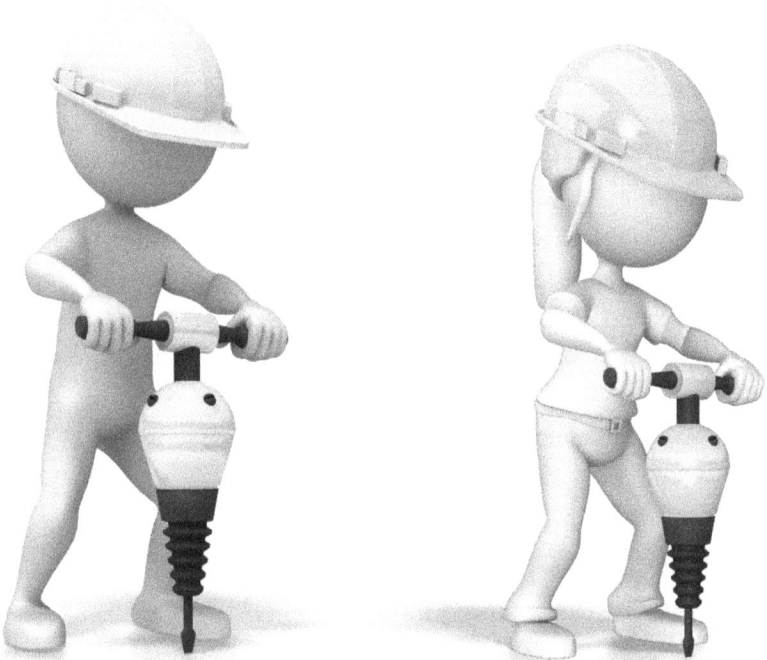

You Need to Drill Down into Pioneering Leadership to Go Deeper

This book offers a Framework that you can use to understand and implement Pioneering Leadership. You can take what you've learnt and apply the principles immediately.

Chapter 9

There is so much more to learn about Pioneering Leadership, you could study to Ph.D. level and still not know all there is to know about it. It is possible to drill down to deeper and deeper levels to gain mastery, but Pioneering Leadership is fundamentally about application and implementation, not about theory, it is about creating a better future.

If you seek to use Pioneering Leadership where others are involved, you need to communicate with and educate them about it. You might need to explore whether you or others are natural Pioneering Leaders or not, or whether you already have Pioneering Leadership inclinations. There are assessment tools that can enable you to do this.

You've done well to get to this point in the book. Over many years, I've seen many highly intelligent and successful people dismiss Pioneering Leadership and carry on with their business as usual, whatever that is, yet these same people will often follow Pioneering Leaders as soon as others start to follow them too. You could become the leader that others follow.

Pioneering Leadership is the most powerful strategy on earth, that offers unlimited possibility, potential and opportunity and can enable you to:

1. Make the seemingly impossible, possible.
2. Solve difficult problems in unique ways.
3. Compete against tough competition and win.
4. Create and exploit exciting opportunities.
5. Achieve extraordinary things.
6. Drive progress and move the human race forward.

If you want to do any of these things, to discover and create better ways and things, and break out the box, blaze new trails, break the mould, change the game or disrupt to create a better future; better lives and careers, better business and organisations, better communities and countries and a better world, I'd love to help you. Use Pioneering Leadership wisely and as a force for good.

Pioneering™
LEADERSHIP ACADEMY
CREATING A BETTER FUTURE

"Helping you to embrace the immense power of Pioneering Leadership."

There are many resources to support you, visit our website:
www.PioneeringLeadership.com

www.JonathanBlain.com
Jonathan@JonathanBlain.com

"In everything that I do, I seek to make a difference, to be a force for good, to discover and use wisdom, love and imagination, and to help others to achieve more, be more, do more, have more of things that matter, know more, make a bigger difference and create a better future."

241

Keynote Presentation

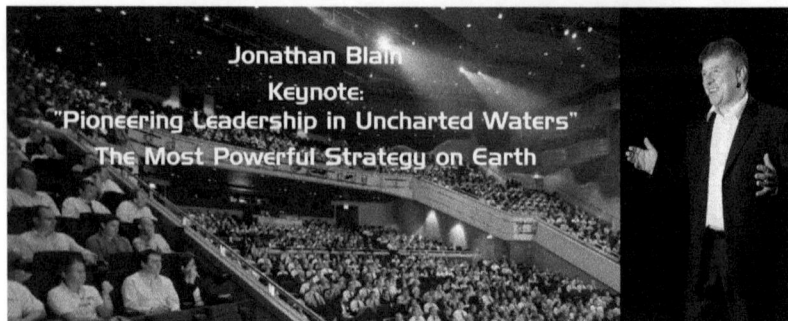

Jonathan Blain Speaks at Seminars Conferences and Events Worldwide

Boardroom Briefing

Consultancy/Coaching/Mentoring

Complete 1:1 Pioneering Leadership personal support to meet the needs of senior executives, teams and major organisations worldwide, including brainstorming, vision development, innovation, creativity, inspiration, imagination, intuition, free/divergent thinking, new approaches, dreaming up and creating new ideas, products, strategies, plans, ventures, solutions, possibilities and opportunities, solving problems and challenges and responses to the Fourth Industrial Revolution.

Pioneering Leadership in Uncharted Waters Program

The Pioneering Leadership in Uncharted Waters Program, follows on from the book and enables you to take Pioneering Leadership to a deeper level and to apply it to an objective / situation of your choice.

The program is designed to support pioneering leadership champions and master practitioners to achieve a specific Pioneering Leadership objectives.

1. Master Classes

2. Online Resources / E-Learning

3. Tools + Techniques

4. Workshops

5. Pioneering Leadership Assessments

Big Problem / Challenge Initiative

Helps organisations to use Pioneering Leadership to solve some of the world's biggest problems and challenges.

Pioneering Ventures

Advises and Supports pioneering enterprises / ventures with disruption. Involvement may include equity partnerships and non-executive directorships.

Partnerships

Partnerships with leading business schools and educational establishments worldwide.

"The truth matters; it is worth searching for. The most important thing to discover is what is important and what isn't, and what is right and what is wrong, what is good and what is bad, what is possible and what is not, what could be and what should be."

Chapter 10

The Authors Back Story

Why I Wrote This Book and Became a Servant Of Humanity

Chapter 10

Please feel free to skip this chapter if you are short on time. My backstory is not particularly short or simple, but it explains my Pioneering Leadership credentials, and why you might choose to trust me as your Pioneering Leadership guide, and also why I became a Servant For Humanity, driven to make a difference in the world.

My story is a mixture of ordinary and extraordinary, of struggle and overcoming adversity, failure and setbacks, developing deep curiosity, questioning things, exploring and searching for answers and adventure, e.g. undertakings involving risk and uncertainty in the hope of positive outcomes with the expectation of excitement. I've had visions and foresight and sought to turn them into reality and experienced explosions of ideas and times of immense creativity and innovation. I've made and lost tens of millions, become a best-selling author of 14 books / $3.8m+ sales, appeared in the local, national and international media on countless occasions and had my work endorsed by many top leaders. This Apple advert resonates with me:

"Here's to the crazy ones. The misfits. The rebels. The troublemakers. The round pegs in the square holes. The ones who see things differently. They're not fond of rules. And they have no respect for the status quo. You can quote them, disagree with them, glorify or vilify them. About the only thing you can't do is ignore them. Because they change things. They push the human race forward. And while some may see them as the crazy ones, we see genius. Because the people who are crazy enough to think they can change the world, are the ones who do."

Rob Siltanen (Writer of this Apple TV advert.)

When I was young, I felt different to most of the other children; I was a deep thinker, I had a big imagination, and I loved pushing myself in things I was interested in, e.g. adventure and other exciting things. I wasn't fond of rules, mainly if I thought they were stupid, and at times it got me into trouble.

There were times when I would test the limits of situations. I particularly liked watching TV and movies, and I decided early on that wanted the exciting, rewarding and adventurous life that I saw people having in the TV programmes and films. I was massively interested in two things, sailing and skateboarding, and I loved the idea of adventure. By the age of 13, I'd miraculously persuaded my parents to let me organise an expedition with my best friend Simon, walking about 120 miles across virtually the entire width of Wales, from Hay-on-Wye to a small village near Milford Haven. When I returned after completing the epic journey, my voice had broken, and I came back more of a man.

By 14, I'd set up my first business, buying watches on a sale or return basis from wholesalers in the Jewellery Quarter of Birmingham in the UK.

I was an early adopter and got into skateboarding when it was virtually unknown in the UK, importing skateboards, equipment and magazines from the USA. With some friends, I co-founded a skateboard club, and as the craze gathered pace, we ended up with over 1700 members. We gained sponsorship from TSB Bank and persuaded a local leisure centre to hand over a part of their car park as our skateboard area. We were able to buy some expensive professional skateboard ramps, and we even had the professional Hobie Skateboard Team from the USA come to our car park. We featured on the national UK TV programme, Nationwide.

My father was in the clothing business; his company had designed, manufactured and imported some skateboard clothing. While still at school, I put on my best suit, I went to visit the purchasing manager of a large local department store and sold them a load of clothing.

I started to think about a career and the possibility of going to university, but nothing seemed to excite me. At the time, a TV programme called Dallas was a big thing, which was all about a rich family in the oil business in Dallas. In my naive youth, I had in mind becoming the rich boss in big business, but I could see that school leavers stood no chance of being successful applying for the boss's job. Then one day, the stars in the heavens seemed to align, I saw an advert in one of the national papers for a 3 ½ year commission in the Royal Navy as a Royal Naval Officer.

The fictional character James Bond was a Royal Naval Officer, as was Prince Philip, Prince Charles and Prince Andrew. If it was good enough for them, it would be good enough for me. I loved the sea, boats of all forms including ships, and I loved the idea of high standards, serving Queen and Country, with the possibility of travelling the world, being involved in the widest range of activities. Being a Royal Naval Seaman Officer ticked all the boxes for me, the only problem was that it was incredibly difficult to get an offer to join. I'd have to compete against boys from top public schools and top universities.

There was a long and detailed application process that culminated in attending a two-day assessment centre called the Admiralty Interview Board. Selection involved written tests, participating in leadership exercises with ropes, planks of wood and a pool of cold water, and some interviews, ending up with an interview with a Senior Royal Naval Officer, a School's Headmaster and a Psychologist.

With zero support from my school and teachers, I'd prepared well, and was amazed to be offered a place to start training at Britannia Royal Naval College in Dartmouth, about a year after Prince Andrew had attended, which incidentally was where the Queen met Prince Philip.

They told us there were 20,000 applicants for approximately 180 places, and of those, only six of us were on the 3 ½ year commission, and of those, I was the only non-graduate. The 3 ½ year commission was an experiment, which presented the Royal Navy with some unique challenges, to get us trained in complicated things like warships, seamanship and navigation quickly enough to get productive work out of us. Their solution was to cut our training time in half, yet the exams we had to pass remained the same as everyone else. This accelerated learning and progression meant that I became the youngest compliment officer in the Royal Navy, doing a proper job, rather than being an Officer Under Training, this suited me fine.

My colleagues on the 3 1/2-year commission were all high calibre; one ended up a Rear Admiral, another a Commodore, and another the MD of Land Rover and CEO of the massive global digger company JCB. I believe who you associate and mix with has a significant impact on what you achieve in your life and career, throughout my career, I've rubbed shoulders with and worked with many super high achievers. I found most of my Royal Navy colleagues to be uplifting. It is never too late to upgrade the people you mix and associate with. Positive can do, and wise people, are likely to lift you up and inspire you, while negative no-hopers are likely to try and pull you down and wear you down. I believe it matters more where you are going than where you are at any time in your career and life. Developing personal philosophy became very important to me.

At a young age, I had many incredible adventures and colossal responsibility, gaining the equivalent of a warship driving license in my early twenties, which meant that I'd be in charge on the bridge of the warship responsible for the entire ship and everyone within it during my watches. I was involved in the cold war and was twice appointed to HMS Coventry immediately before the Falklands war. She sailed for war the day after I was appointed to her, and was hit and sunk by an Argentine bomb with the loss of 19 lives and 30 were injured. Life can be short, so I think we all need to make the most of it.

I had a vast variety of experiences; one day I could be hosting foreign dignitaries and diplomats at a cocktail party, another day I could be running a gunnery shoot. I dealt with the ships correspondence and cash, boarded and inspected fishing boats as a British Sea Fisheries Officer, making arrests and supported prosecutions. I took part in search and rescue operations, chased Russian warships and took part in anti-terrorist exercises with the SBS, the Royal Marines Special Forces. While at Britannia Royal Naval College I was in the room next to the Prince of Tonga, I once gave him a lift in my car, and he is now the

Chapter 10

King. While doing warfare training, I became friends with a Malaysian Naval Officer, Ahmad Kamarulzaman Hj Ahmad Badaruddin he is now an Admiral and the Chief (Head) of the Royal Malaysian Navy.

Shortly after I joined the Royal Navy, the highly successful film "An Officer and a Gentleman" came out, starring Richard Gere as a US Navy Officer. There have been many times in my life where real-life situations that I have been in, would be worthy of being made into films.

When my 3 ½ years were up in the Royal Navy, it was the oil industry that I turned to, securing a job with the Mobil Oil Corporation, which was then the world's fourth-largest company. After ten exciting years, it was time to spread my wings again but this time as an entrepreneur, business owner and author.

While in the Royal Navy and at Mobil Oil Corporation, I found that I could comply with rules, but I always had a burning desire for improvement. Nothing would be more pleasurable than positive change, growth, evolution, advancement, improvement, dreaming up new ideas, new strategies and new approaches, implementing them and getting game-changing results. Over those years I had many bosses, some were supportive, and others weren't. Sometimes my ideas delivered spectacular results, and sometimes they didn't. I loved the variety of roles I got to undertake in the Royal Navy and at Mobil. It always amazed me how versatile we human beings can be if we need to or want to. In Mobil, I spent time in customer service, sales, investment buying land and redeveloping petrol stations, as a business analyst doing executive reports and as an area manager running a group of high volume petrol stations across north-west London. While pitted against career salesman; my creativity helped me to win the incentive for the best salesman, which resulted in a 5-star luxury holiday to Jamaica. It also helped me to create the highest performing Mobil Petrol Station area in the UK. While in head office, I loved the arrival of computers and ended up seconded to a pan-European project implementing the software system SAP.

I might not be a fantastic computer techie, but I found that I was very good at seeing the big picture and anticipating what might happen in the future. It was while working for Mobil that I took a trip to Berlin to see my then girlfriend's (now wife's) sister. Her boyfriend introduced me to the internet, which resulted in me setting up websites for the multiple businesses I was to create. It was the early pioneering days when most people had not even heard of the internet. Through one of these websites, I was able to win a contract to write first one book, and then seven more books on the computer system SAP for Macmillan, which was then the biggest computer book publisher in the world. My flagship book was in their top ten bestsellers for an entire year and one month was their third bestselling book out of over 800 titles.

SAP software was then one of the world's most advanced and sophisticated computer systems, used by the world's largest and most prestigious organisations. My books generated over $3.8m in sales and were used all over the world. Seeing a problem in the ERP computer software market of which SAP was a part, I succeeded in persuading the Secretary of State to grant permission to establish an Institute to raise standards. SAP and most of their major competitors supported the launch of the Institute. SAP hosted the Institute's launch event at their UK headquarters.

That book led to me establishing a recruitment company relating to people with SAP computing skills and experience, which in turn enabled me to enter into a joint venture recruitment business with Hays Plc which was then a FTSE 100 company. I don't think many private individuals have been successful in going into business partnership with a FTSE 100 company.

I began to recognise what pioneering leadership could enable you to achieve, I had the vision, saw the opportunity and in just nine months made myself worth over £20m by floating my company and attaining the largest ever IPO at the time, on the OFEX stock market in the UK.

My passion for sailing took me from small sailing dinghies to bigger yachts, which I shared with my best friend from my school days, Simon, who I walked across Wales with when we were just 13 years old. We had countless adventures together, the most dramatic of which was in 1990 during the two-handed trans-Atlantic yacht race. Our yacht developed severe faults, leaking so severely that the floorboards were floating around on the inside of the boat, the entire steering wheel had broken off, and the rudder had jammed on full lock, the main structural bulkhead had cracked, and fittings had ripped out of the deck leaving a hole. My Royal Naval Officer training came into its own as the situation deteriorated, which resulted in surviving mountainous seas and gale force winds in icy cold seas, and ultimately a record-breaking air-sea rescue that made it into the national papers and on TV.

That experience made me question the design and construction of modern production boats at the time. I had the vision to create something better, ahead of its time. I contacted all the leading yacht designers, and most of them didn't get it, but one did, a designer called Ed Dubois, who went on to become one of the world's most famous super-yacht designers.

With very little money, I set about doing what I had always done when I had limited resources, and that was to become resourceful. At the time, one of the UK's top yachting magazines had been designing what they considered to be the perfect cruising yacht. My new yacht was the antithesis to this, light displacement, long waterline length, very fast and good looking. In the years since, many of the features pioneered by my design have become mainstream.

I have so many stories and experiences, it would take a series of books to capture them all, but what links them together is that I was practising Pioneering Leadership, without realising it, because it reflected who I indeed was; an Extreme Game-Changer, a mould-breaker and a pioneer. I see the big picture and the detail when most others don't; I have a massive curiosity and a desire to learn, to discover the truth, make the connections and figure out new ways of solving problems, creating opportunities and achieving extraordinary things.

My early experiences in the Royal Navy and with the Mobil Oil Corporation helped me to thrive in different environments and roles, and I recognised that there are principles about how to achieve things that apply to anything, regardless of what specific role or task or issue is current.

I have since written many books, which have been endorsed by many top leaders, from different areas. These include nine heads of UK top 1000 companies including Apple, Sony, Carphone Warehouse, St James's Place, one of the Co-Founders of global software giant SAP and entrepreneurs including Sir John Timpson and businesswomen of the year, Dawn Gibbins, MBE. Other endorsements have come from The Director General of the Institute of Directors, the First Sea Lord of the Royal Navy and even the ex-President of Luxembourg.

I've had involvement in many different things including childcare and child education. I've spoken about it on BBC Breakfast and at the House of Commons. I've talked about people who make the world a better place on BBC News 24, in fact, I have been in most of the UK's major national newspapers and on local, national and international TV and Radio on numerous occasions.

Mine has been a career and life journey of massive highs and lows, extraordinary achievements and countless failures and struggles, but each has been a learning experience. Over time, my ego gave way to humility, and I became a servant of humanity.

I developed a deep interest in leadership and created the Leadership Master Class Series, which I believe is still the world's most comprehensive video-based leadership education on leadership excellence. In this programme, I interviewed top leaders and thought leaders from Business, The Military, Academia and the Not for Profit Sector as well as many Thought Leaders.

As I embarked on a journey of personal development, growth and ultimately transformation, I learnt about many different assessment tools and was eventually able to be diagnosed as an "Extreme Game Changer" GC Index. The GC Index, based on credible academic research, identifies the wired-in characteristics and traits of "game changers" like me. The research states that not everyone can be a game-changer, but everyone can contribute towards game-changing teams. The truth is that as human beings we are all different, but we can be categorised into types with common attributes; the world needs each type, diversity provides an important function, we all need each other. Great leaders can lead diverse teams, combining depth and breadth of skills, attributes, beliefs and sometimes values.

I don't dispute this academic research, we all are who we are. You can't inherently be a game-changer, if you are not a game changer, it is like trying to be someone you are not. However, I am a game changer, but I've successfully done many roles that don't sit comfortably with who I am because I followed a process. Typically driving a ship around the ocean doesn't require game-changer skills, equally trying out risky game-changing in areas of health and safety on petrol stations with thousands of litres of highly flammable fuel is probably not a good idea. A big corporations couldn't exist if people didn't comply with company policies and procedures and legal requirements. If I could do these things, why can't other people who are not game changers, do game-changing things and achieve game-changing results?

When I think back through my life, I can think of many examples of where I have helped other people to achieve extraordinary things by adopting pioneering leadership strategies, in niche areas including writing CV's, marketing and selling yourself to get jobs that you thought were beyond you and in achieving organisational and personal success.

In 1995, I was on holiday yachting on the south coast of the UK with my wife Jenny, when I met an 18-year-old girl sailing around Britain. We became friends, and she shared a dream to take part in a trans-Atlantic yacht race called the Mini Transat. To take part in the race, she needed a yacht, yet she had virtually no money. She wrote thousands of letters looking for sponsorship, but to no avail. At the bleakest point, when all hope seemed like being lost, I was able to find a way of helping her to get that yacht. I also persuaded the Royal Southampton Yacht Club to give her honorary membership. They twice turned down my suggestion before eventually succumbing and making the offer. Approximately ten years later, the BBC paid for me to travel to Falmouth in the South Coast of the UK, put me up in a hotel and interviewed me on the deck of this young girl's high-tech trimaran yacht. This young girl, Ellen MacArthur, had become the fastest person to sail around the world and became the UK's youngest Dame. There were said to 8000 people there to welcome her on her triumphant return, with TV crews from all over the world.

Her success was down to her and her team and a great number of people along the way, but what is certain is that before she was well known and famous, I saw the possibility of her achieving her dreams. I helped, supported and encouraged her at a critical time, and the result was a truly extraordinary achievement. Small insignificant things can make all the difference.

My lovely wife Jenny has been the most significant influence on my life, she is full of love and kindness and is a genius at educating young nursery age children, and giving them the best start in life. In 1991, she established the incredible and unique Denning Montessori Nursery School in an idyllic rural location, just outside Henley on Thames in the UK. See www.DenningMontessoriSchool.com. Her school is all about being leaders in nurture, quality over quantity, and unlike many nursery owners, she is in the classroom, the outdoor learning environment and Forest School teaching almost every day. She was a finalist in the Nursery Personality of the Year Award and given a national award as one of the Five Most Inspirational People in the Childcare Sector in the UK. I love helping out in the school and am inspired by the brilliance of Pioneering Leader, Dr Maria Montessori, who established the Montessori method of education.

In an interview with Barbara Walters, the founders of Google, Pioneering Leaders Larry Page and Sergei Brin, credited their success, not to their education at Stanford, but to their early Montessori education.

Chapter 10

Jeff Bezos, founder of Amazon, is also a big fan of Montessori, and has committed to spending $2billion to create and operate a national network of Montessori preschools in the USA.

For many years, I helped Jenny establish and run a club for Montessori teachers from all over the world, and establish a company which made a range of innovative furniture units for Montessori schools and equipment and sold Montessori software that Jenny helped create.

As I have grown older and reflected on my life as a polymath with so many varied experiences including many highs and lows, I've learnt to see things from many different angles and perspectives. The arrogance of my youth gave way to humility, and the illusion and glamour commonplace in the modern world started to fade away and reveal glimpses of the truth. Once you see a doorway to the truth about things, it opens up a well of curiosity that can only be satisfied by the exploration of things that are interesting and important. I experienced a personal tipping point where my life purpose revealed itself:

"In everything that I do, I seek to make a difference, to be a force for good, to discover and use wisdom, love and imagination, and to help others to achieve more, be more, do more, have more of what matters, know more, and make a bigger difference. Through my work, I intend to be an agent of positive change and create an enabling, uplifting and positive revolution in the world, where people get to see, think and act differently, so they can make things better for themselves, others, future generations and the entire world."

Reflecting on my past, I recognised that I had done and achieved many things that were far removed from my natural skills, nature and personality. I realised that it is also possible for anyone prepared to follow a Pioneering Leadership strategy and process, even if they are not a natural Pioneering Leader to achieve game-changing results. It was this ah-ha moment of awareness that made me create the Pioneering Leadership Academy (www.PioneeringLeadership.com), write this book, and create the Pioneering Leadership in Uncharted Waters Framework for you and others to use, so that you too can have the possibility of achieving extraordinary things (if you haven't already), without being a natural Pioneering Leader. All you've got to do is to use the Pioneering Leadership in Uncharted Waters Framework. If it seems too difficult to do it yourself, you can identify any natural Pioneering Leaders in your organisation or team, or hire external ones like me to help you.

I can see that Pioneering Leadership is the most powerful strategy on earth, that can unlock unlimited possibility, potential and opportunity. It can help you to:

1. Make the seemingly impossible possible.
2. Solve difficult problems and challenges in unique ways.
3. Create and exploit exciting opportunities.
4. Compete against tough competition and win.
5. Achieve extraordinary things.
6. Drive progress and move the human race forward.

Sharing this epiphany and helping others to access these benefits of Pioneering Leadership is now a significant part of my life purpose.

The needs in the world at every level: individual, group, business, organisational, community, national, international and global are colossal. Pioneering Leadership can help solve the biggest problems and challenges at every level and also offers the greatest opportunities.

ACKNOWLEDGEMENTS AND
SPECIAL THANKS

Irfan Idrees

This is the second book project that I have done with Irfan. Irfan has brought experience and expertise to the book design process for both printing and e-book distribution. It has been a joy to work with Irfan, he has always been incredibly helpful, and we've formed an effective partnership.

Paul Barclay

Paul came up with the splash writing for my logo. He is a good friend and a talented artist, illustration, designer and sign writer. His incredible Paul Barclay Brand continues to grow.If you happen to visit Dartmouth in the UK, I suggest you visit his shop and studio in 1 Oxford Street and mention my name!

www.PaulBarclayDesigns.com

Michael Mayhew-Arnold

Michael is a barrister, author, journalist and head of legal for major international organisations. Michael has been a great friend and incredibly supportive of me and the writing of this book, and I'd like to thank him for everything.

Acknowledgements and Special Thanks

Simon Chance

Simon has been my best friend since we were nine years old; he has been like a brother to me, and we have been on many adventures together. His friendship and support continually remind me of how important good friendships are in our lives. Good friends are priceless, they make life worth living, it is great to have them, but we also need to remember that we need to try and be good friends to others too.

My Family

The year this book was written, we celebrated my mother's eightieth birthday. Happy birthday mum! To celebrate, we spent two weeks together yachting in Mallorca and Menorca, which helped clear my mind to write this book, and reconnected me to the idea of uncharted waters.

I'd like to thank my entire family for their love, support and understanding with a special mention to my lovely wife Jenny, (it was our 25th wedding anniversary in 2018), our beautiful daughters, Kezia, Xanthe and Talia, my mum Neva and my sister, Deborah.

Index

A

Al-Qaeda 19
Amazon 15, 39, 41, 44, 256
Annie Get Your Gun 217
Apple 15, 17, 10, 41, 44, 45, 166, 246, 253
Aron Ralston 183
Artificial Intelligence 93
Arts University Bournemouth 94, 95
automation 93

B

BBC 136, 160, 161, 253, 255
Arun Bedi 4, 10
behavioural biases 180
Best Practice 3, 155, 159
Bill Gates 15, 48, 58, 140, 166
Jonathan Blain 1, 2, 10, 28, 242
Blue Ocean Strategy 17, 104
Britannia Royal Naval College 97, 248, 249

C

Charles Dickens 146
Clayton M. Christensen 17

D

Dalai Lama 72
David Eagleman 21, 77, 78
Disruptive Innovation 17, 67, 104
DNA 15, 41, 46
Doug Goodale 183

E

Einstein 16, 19, 3, 18, 46, 47, 48, 58, 81, 109, 118, 130, 140, 161, 162, 187,

Index

luddite 23, 52

M

Mahatma Gandhi 17, 85
Malcolm Stamper 203
Marcel Proust 60
Maria Montessori 255
Mark Zuckerberg 15, 48, 140, 161, 166
Martin M. Broadwell 117
Michael Dell 166
Mobil Oil Corporation 28, 126, 250, 253
Montessori 255, 256
Musk Electric Jet 50

N

Nelson Mandela 17, 58, 80
Non-Arts based creativity 95
non-disruptive 13, 32, 41, 189
Normalisation 20, 67

O

Olympic Games 87
Nathan Ott 31
Out The Box Thinking 3

P

paradigm shift 223
Paul Howard-Jones 100
Percy Spencer 214
Pete Goss 161
Plato 21, 72, 73, 74, 75, 77
polymath 50
Professor Everett M. Rogers 68
Professor Klaus Schwab 189

R

Renée Mauborgne 17

Lightning Source UK Ltd.
Milton Keynes UK
UKHW021832220920
370332UK00008B/226

9 781905 243228